The Heart of God

*Praying the Scriptures
to Expand Your Vision*

Kenneth Boa

BakerBooks
Grand Rapids, Michigan

© 2005 by Kenneth Boa

Published by Baker Books
a division of Baker Publishing Group
P.O. Box 6287, Grand Rapids, MI 49516-6287

Printed in the United States of America

Library of Congress Cataloging-in-Publication Data
Boa, Kenneth.
    The heart of God : praying the Scriptures to expand your vision
/ Kenneth Boa.
        p.   cm.
    ISBN 0-8010-6549-6 (pbk.)
    1. Prayer—Christianity. 2. Prayers. 3. Bible—Prayers. I. Title.
BV210.3.B62 2005
242'.722—dc22   2005006183

Published in partnership with World Vision
34834 Weyerhaeuser Way South, P.O. Box 9716
Federal Way, WA 98063 USA

Scripture is taken from the *Holy Bible*, New Living Translation, copyright
© 1996. Used by permission of Tyndale House Publishers, Inc., Wheaton,
Illinois 60189. All rights reserved.

In some instances, Scripture was modified by the author to personalize the
reading with permission from Tyndale House Publishers.

Italics in biblical quotations indicate emphasis added by the author.

"Let my heart be broken by the things that break the heart of God."

Dr. Robert Pierce,
founder of World Vision

Contents

Introduction

People who follow Christ desire to know the heart of God through Scripture and prayer, but many are frustrated with their Bible reading and dissatisfied with their prayer lives. *The Heart of God* is designed to help you overcome these obstacles by enriching the quality of your time with the Lord. Combining Scripture reading and prayer, you will enhance your devotional life and move toward genuine understanding and wisdom.

Over the centuries, people have tended to two extremes in prayer: excessive form (repetition to the point of losing meaning) and excessive freedom (praying whatever comes to mind). *The Heart of God* encourages a combination of form and freedom. It modifies biblical passages into personal prayers and guides you through several kinds of prayer. But within this structure, it also stresses flexibility, personalization, and spontaneous response.

The Heart of God is simple to use, and it gives you the advantage of praying Scripture back to God. Because it is Scripture, you can be confident that these are things the Lord would want you to pray. This promotes the process of cleansing and transforming you into a new person "by changing the way you think" (Romans 12:2).

By using this daily guide to prayer and renewal, you will achieve greater skill in the art of prayer. You will be better equipped to worship the Lord in spirit and truth (John 4:24), and you will be better prepared to love him by serving others (Matthew 22:37–40; Ephesians 2:10).

Each day consists of these forms of prayer:

Praise and Worship: Focusing on the heart of God

Personal Examination: Focusing on my own heart

Commitment: Devoting myself to God

Personal Concerns: Cultivating a sensitive heart

Concerns for Others: Developing a heart for others

Prayer of Thanksgiving: Assuming an attitude of humility and grace

Concluding Prayer: Experiencing God's love and favor

Be sure to use the prayer prompts that follow the prayers and affirmations so that you do not merely read the prayers. Instead, personalize them so that they can become part of your own thoughts and experience and expand your vision for your own needs and the needs of the world.

The First Month

Day 1

Praise and Worship

I have been chosen to know you, believe in you, and understand that you alone are God. There is no other God; there never has been and never will be. (Isaiah 43:10)

This is what the Lord, Israel's King and Redeemer, the Lord Almighty, says: "I am the First and the Last; there is no other God." (Isaiah 44:6)

Pause to express your thoughts of praise and worship.

Personal Examination

What are mere mortals, that you should make so much of us? For you examine us every morning and test us every moment. (Job 7:17–18)

Ask the Spirit to search your heart and reveal any areas of unconfessed sin. Acknowledge these to the Lord and thank him for his forgiveness.

Commitment

He must become greater and greater, and I must become less and less. (John 3:30)

You are the true vine, and your Father is the gardener. He cuts off every branch that doesn't produce fruit, and he prunes the branches that do bear fruit so they will produce even more. May I remain in you, and you in me. For a branch cannot produce fruit if it is severed from the vine, and I cannot be fruitful apart from you. (John 15:1–2, 4)

Pause to add your own prayers for commitment and renewal.

Personal Concerns

May I fight a good fight, finish the race, and remain faithful. And may the prize await me—the crown of righteousness that the Lord, the righteous Judge, will give me on that great day of his return. And the prize is not just for me but for all who eagerly look forward to his glorious return. (2 Timothy 4:7–8)

Love and Compassion

Pause to ask for the grace of greater love and compassion for others. Pray that you will become a more Christlike person who considers the needs of others above your own, knowing that God is your provider and sustainer.

Concerns for Others

I pray that you will give me the right words as I boldly explain your secret plan. (Ephesians 6:19)

Christian Witness

Pray on behalf of the people you personally know who have not yet entered into the joy of a personal relationship with Jesus. Intercede for your unsaved relatives, neighbors, co-workers, and friends.

Prayer of Thanksgiving

I will have peace in you. Here on earth I will have many trials and sorrows. But I will take heart, because you have overcome the world. (John 16:33)

I am chosen by God and sent out to preach his Good News. I am among those who have been called to belong to Jesus Christ. (Romans 1:1, 6)

Pause to offer your own expressions of thanksgiving.

Concluding Prayer

May our Lord Jesus Christ and God our Father, who loved us and in his special favor gave us everlasting comfort and good hope, comfort my heart and give me strength in every good thing I do and say. (2 Thessalonians 2:16–17)

God is the blessed and only almighty God, the King of kings and Lord of lords. He alone can never die, and he lives in light so brilliant that no human can approach him. No one has ever seen him, nor ever will. To him be honor and power forever. Amen. (1 Timothy 6:15b–16)

Day 2

Praise and Worship

Heaven is your throne, and the earth is your footstool. Your hands have made both heaven and earth, and they are yours. (Isaiah 66:1–2a)

It was your hand that laid the foundations of the earth. The palm of your right hand spread out the heavens above. You spoke, and they came into being. (Isaiah 48:13)

Pause to express your thoughts of praise and worship.

Personal Examination

Search me, O God, and know my heart; test me and know my thoughts. Point out anything in me that offends you, and lead me along the path of everlasting life. (Psalm 139:23–24)

Ask the Spirit to search your heart and reveal any areas of unconfessed sin. Acknowledge these to the Lord and thank him for his forgiveness.

Commitment

May you, LORD my God, be with me as you were with my ancestors; may you never forsake me. May you give me the desire to do your will in everything and to obey all the commands, laws, and regulations that you gave my ancestors. May people all over the earth know that the LORD is God and that there is no other god. And may I always be faithful to the LORD my God. May I always obey his laws and commands, just as I am doing today. (1 Kings 8:57–58, 60–61)

May I listen to you who know right from wrong and cherish your law in my heart. May I not be afraid of people's scorn or their slanderous talk. (Isaiah 51:7)

Pause to add your own prayers for commitment and renewal.

Personal Concerns

Please help me never to tell a lie and give me neither poverty nor riches! Give me just enough to satisfy my needs. For if I grow rich, I may deny you and say, "Who is the LORD?" And if I am too poor, I may steal and thus insult God's holy name. (Proverbs 30:8–9)

Faithfulness as a Steward

Pause to ask that God would empower you to become a more faithful and effective steward with all that he has entrusted to your care. Since he has given you a stewardship of talents, treasure, truth, time, love and compassion, ask that you would use these gifts with fidelity in his service.

Concerns for Others

Give to everyone what you owe them: Pay your taxes and import duties, and give respect and honor to all to whom it is due. (Romans 13:7)

Government

Lift up those in local, state, and national government, and pray that those in positions of authority would look to God for wisdom in their decisions and practice.

Prayer of Thanksgiving

I will give thanks to the LORD, for he is good! His faithful love endures forever. I praise the LORD for his great love and for all his wonderful deeds to us. He satisfies the thirsty and fills the hungry with good things. (Psalm 107:1, 8–9)

Pause to offer your own expressions of thanksgiving.

Concluding Prayer

There are secret things that belong to you, LORD God, but the revealed things belong to us and our descendants forever, so that we may obey these words of the law. (Deuteronomy 29:29)

We praise you, LORD, for all your glorious power. With music and singing we celebrate your mighty acts. (Psalm 21:13)

Day 3

Praise and Worship

He created everything there is. Nothing exists that he didn't make. Life itself was in him, and this life gives light to everyone. (John 1:3–4)

The Lord Jesus is the one who is holy and true. He is the one who has the key of David. He opens doors, and no one can shut them; he shuts doors, and no one can open them. (Revelation 3:7)

Pause to express your thoughts of praise and worship.

Personal Examination

When I sin against the LORD, I may be sure that my sin will find me out. (Numbers 32:23)

Ask the Spirit to search your heart and reveal any areas of unconfessed sin. Acknowledge these to the Lord and thank him for his forgiveness.

Commitment

I once thought all these things were so very important, but now I consider them worthless because of what Christ has done. Yes, everything else is worthless when compared with the priceless gain of knowing Christ Jesus my Lord. I have discarded everything else, counting it all as garbage, so that I may have Christ and become one with him. I no longer count on my own goodness or my ability to obey God's law, but I trust Christ to save me. For God's way of making us right with himself depends on faith. (Philippians 3:7–9)

Pause to add your own prayers for commitment and renewal.

Personal Concerns

May I be an example to all believers in what I teach, in the way I live, in my love, my faith, and my purity. (1 Timothy 4:12)

Family and Ministry

Pause to lift up your family, your career, and your ministry before the Lord. Ask that you would have the privilege of sharing Christ with others and helping people grow in their knowledge of him.

Concerns for Others

Jesus traveled through all the cities and villages of that area, teaching in the synagogues and announcing the Good News about the Kingdom. And wherever he went, he healed people of every sort of disease and illness. He felt great pity for the crowds that came, because their problems were so great and they didn't know where to go for help. They were like sheep without a shepherd. He said to his disciples, "The harvest is so great, but the workers are so few. So pray to the Lord who is in charge of the harvest; ask him to send out more workers for his fields." (Matthew 9:35–38)

Missions

Intercede for national and world missions, and pray that those who have dedicated their lives to the fulfillment of the Great Commission will be strengthened, encouraged, and empowered.

Prayer of Thanksgiving

I am overwhelmed with joy in the Lord my God! For he has dressed me with the clothing of salvation and draped me in a robe of righteousness. I am like a bridegroom in his wedding suit or a bride with her jewels. The Sovereign Lord will show his justice to the nations of the world. Everyone will praise him! His righteousness will be like a garden in early spring, filled with young plants springing up everywhere. (Isaiah 61:10)

I wait quietly before God, for my salvation comes from him. He alone is my rock and my salvation, my fortress where I will never be shaken. (Psalm 62:1–2)

Pause to offer your own expressions of thanksgiving.

Concluding Prayer

O Sovereign Lord! You have made the heavens and earth by your great power. Nothing is too hard for you! You are loving and kind to thousands, though children suffer for their parents' sins. You are the great and powerful God, the Lord Almighty. You have all wisdom and do great and mighty miracles. You are very aware of the conduct of all people, and you reward them according to their deeds. (Jeremiah 32:17–19)

Day 4

Praise and Worship

Who is able to advise the Spirit of the LORD? Who knows enough to be his teacher or counselor? Has the LORD ever needed anyone's advice? Does he need instruction about what is good or what is best? No, for all the nations of the world are nothing in comparison with him. They are but a drop in the bucket, dust on the scales. The nations of the world are as nothing to him. In his eyes they are less than nothing—mere emptiness and froth. To whom, then, can we compare God? What image might we find to resemble him? (Isaiah 40:13–15, 17–18)

Pause to express your thoughts of praise and worship.

Personal Examination

Our earthly fathers disciplined us for a few years, doing the best they knew how. But God's discipline is always right and good for us because it means we will share in his holiness. No discipline is enjoyable while it is happening—it is painful! But afterward there will be a quiet harvest of right living for those who are trained in this way. So take a new grip with your tired hands and stand firm on your shaky legs. Mark out a straight path for your feet. Then those who follow you, though they are weak and lame, will not stumble and fall but will become strong. (Hebrews 12:10–13)

Ask the Spirit to search your heart and reveal any areas of unconfessed sin. Acknowledge these to the Lord and thank him for his forgiveness.

Commitment

Like Asa, may I do what is pleasing and good in the sight of the LORD my God. (2 Chronicles 14:2)

Like Jehoshaphat, let me be committed to the ways of the LORD and destroy the places of idolatry in my life. (2 Chronicles 17:6)

Pause to add your own prayers for commitment and renewal.

Personal Concerns

"Love the Lord your God with all your heart, all your soul, and all your mind." This is the first and greatest commandment. A second is equally important: "Love your neighbor as yourself." All the other commandments and all the demands of the prophets are based on these two commandments. (Matthew 22:37–40)

Growth in Character
Pause to look to the Lord for the power to stand firm in the spiritual warfare against the world, the flesh, and spiritual forces of wickedness. Ask that you would grow in character and pursue the disciplines of the faith in a spirit of radical dependence upon him.

Concerns for Others

May I show more and more of God's mercy, peace, and love. (Jude 22)

World Affairs

Lift up the needs of the poor and the hungry, the oppressed and the persecuted. Pray for those in positions of authority and ask for the blessings of peace rather than conflict.

Prayer of Thanksgiving

This is the Good News for the people of Israel—that there is peace with God through Jesus Christ, who is Lord of all. And he ordered us to preach everywhere and to testify that Jesus is ordained of God to be the judge of all—the living and the dead. He is the one all the prophets testified about, saying that everyone who believes in him will have their sins forgiven through his name. (Acts 10:36, 42–43)

Pause to offer your own expressions of thanksgiving.

Concluding Prayer

I rejoice in your word like one who finds a great treasure. I hate and abhor all falsehood, but I love your law. Those who love your law have great peace and do not stumble. I long for your salvation, Lord, so I have obeyed your commands. I have obeyed your decrees, and I love them very much. Yes, I obey your commandments and decrees, because you know everything I do. (Psalm 119:162–63, 165–68)

Day 5

Praise and Worship

Then I looked again, and I heard the singing of thousands and millions of angels around the throne and the living beings and the elders. And they sang in a mighty chorus: "The Lamb is worthy—the Lamb who was killed. He is worthy to receive power and riches and wisdom and strength and honor and glory and blessing." (Revelation 5:11–12)

Pause to express your thoughts of praise and worship.

Personal Examination

God is so wise and so mighty. Who has ever challenged him successfully? (Job 9:4)

Ask the Spirit to search your heart and reveal any areas of unconfessed sin. Acknowledge these to the Lord and thank him for his forgiveness.

Commitment

May I be careful and watch out for attacks from the Devil, my great enemy. He prowls around like a roaring lion, looking for some victim to devour. I will take a firm stand against him, and be strong in my faith. I remember that my Christian brothers and sisters all over the world are going through the same kind of suffering I am. (1 Peter 5:8–9)

May I stand my ground, putting on the sturdy belt of truth and the body armor of God's righteousness. For shoes, may I put on the peace that comes from the Good News, so that I will be fully prepared. In every battle I will need faith as my shield to stop the fiery arrows aimed at me by Satan. I will put on salvation as my helmet, and take the sword of the Spirit, which is the word of God. I will pray at all times and on every occasion in the power of the Holy Spirit. May I stay alert and be persistent in my prayers for all Christians everywhere. (Ephesians 6:14–18)

Pause to add your own prayers for commitment and renewal.

Personal Concerns

Now that I am old and gray, do not abandon me, O God. Let me proclaim your power to this new generation, your mighty miracles to all who come after me. (Psalm 71:18)

Knowing, Loving, and Trusting God
Pause to ask God for the grace to know and please him. Ask him to enlarge your capacity to love him more and abide wholly in him.

Concerns for Others

Some of us are Jews, some are Gentiles, some are slaves, and some are free. But we have all been baptized into Christ's body by one Spirit, and we have all received the same Spirit. (1 Corinthians 12:13)

Churches and Ministries

Ask God to work on behalf of the people and concerns at your local church. Pray for his blessing and power in the ministries that are engaged in Christian witness, discipleship, education, and those serving people in need.

Prayer of Thanksgiving

I love the LORD because he hears and answers my prayers. Because he bends down and listens, I will pray as long as I have breath! (Psalm 116:1–2)

Give thanks to the God of heaven. His faithful love endures forever. (Psalm 136:26)

Pause to offer your own expressions of thanksgiving.

Concluding Prayer

The LORD has made the heavens his throne; from there he rules over everything. Praise the LORD, you angels of his, you mighty creatures who carry out his plans, listening for each of his commands. Yes, praise the LORD, you armies of angels who serve him and do his will! Praise the LORD, everything he has created, everywhere in his kingdom. As for me—I, too, will praise the LORD. (Psalm 103:19–22)

Day 6

Praise and Worship

Where were you when I laid the foundations of the earth? Tell me, if you know so much. Do you know how its dimensions were determined and who did the surveying? What supports its foundations, and who laid its cornerstone as the morning stars sang together and all the angels shouted for joy? (Job 38:4–7)

I AM THE ONE WHO ALWAYS IS. Just tell them, "I AM has sent me to you." (Exodus 3:14)

Pause to express your thoughts of praise and worship.

Personal Examination

God will not constantly accuse me, nor remain angry forever. He has not punished me for all my sins, nor does he deal with us as we deserve. For his unfailing love toward those who fear him is as great as the height of the heavens above the earth. He has removed our rebellious acts as far away from us as the east is from the west. The LORD is like a father to his children, tender and compassionate to those who fear him. (Psalm 103:9–13)

Ask the Spirit to search your heart and reveal any areas of unconfessed sin. Acknowledge these to the Lord and thank him for his forgiveness.

Commitment

Since I am living now by the Holy Spirit, let me follow the Holy Spirit's leading in every part of my life. (Galatians 5:25)

May God give me a complete understanding of what he wants to do in my life, and make me wise with spiritual wisdom. Then the way I live will always honor and please the Lord, and I will continually do good, kind things for others. All the while, I will learn to know God better and better. (Colossians 1:9–11)

Pause to add your own prayers for commitment and renewal.

Personal Concerns

May I be strong and very courageous; and may I obey all the laws Moses gave. May I not turn away from them, and I will be successful in everything I do. (Joshua 1:7)

Greater Wisdom

Pause to ask God for the grace to develop an eternal perspective on your life and concerns, and that he would renew your mind with his truth. Ask for the power to order your steps with wisdom and skill in each area of life so that you will seek to please him rather than impress others.

Concerns for Others

Hear me, LORD, and have mercy on me. Help me, O LORD. You have turned my mourning into joyful dancing. You have taken away my clothes of mourning and clothed me with joy, that I might sing praises to you and not be silent. O Lord my God, I will give you thanks forever! (Psalm 30:10–12)

Loved Ones

Lift up the members of your immediate family and your extended family. Pray for the spiritual, emotional, and physical concerns of your loved ones.

Prayer of Thanksgiving

The Lord your God is merciful—he will not abandon you or destroy you or forget the solemn covenant he made with your ancestors. (Deuteronomy 4:31)

You, O Lord, are a shield around me, my glory, and the one who lifts my head high. (Psalm 3:3)

Pause to offer your own expressions of thanksgiving.

Concluding Prayer

I know that the Lord saves his anointed king. He will answer him from his holy heaven and rescue him by his great power. Some nations boast of their armies and weapons, but we boast in the Lord our God. (Psalm 20:6–7)

Day 7

Praise and Worship

The LORD is a jealous God, filled with vengeance and wrath. He takes revenge on all who oppose him and furiously destroys his enemies! The LORD is slow to get angry, but his power is great, and he never lets the guilty go unpunished. He displays his power in the whirlwind and the storm. The billowing clouds are the dust beneath his feet. (Nahum 1:2–3)

You are a God who is not only in one place. You can see what we are doing. No one can hide from you. You are everywhere in all the heavens and earth. (Jeremiah 23:23–24)

Pause to express your thoughts of praise and worship.

Personal Examination

"Come now, let us argue this out," says the LORD. "No matter how deep the stain of your sins, I can remove it. I can make you as clean as freshly fallen snow. Even if you are stained as red as crimson, I can make you as white as wool." (Isaiah 1:18)

Ask the Spirit to search your heart and reveal any areas of unconfessed sin. Acknowledge these to the Lord and thank him for his forgiveness.

Commitment

As I obey God, may I not slip back into my old ways of doing evil; I didn't know any better then. But now I must be holy in everything I do, just as God—who chose me to be his child—is holy. For he himself has said, "You must be holy because I am holy." (1 Peter 1:14–16)

You, Lord God, call me to be holy because you are holy. May I not defile myself. I must be holy because you, Lord my God, are holy. (Leviticus 11:44–45; 19:2)

Pause to add your own prayers for commitment and renewal.

Personal Concerns

May I not say, "Today or tomorrow I am going to a certain town and will stay there a year. I will do business there and make a profit." How do I know what will happen tomorrow? For my life is like the morning fog—it's here a little while, then it's gone. May I instead say, "If the Lord wants me to, I will live and do this or that." Otherwise I will be boasting about my own plans, and all such boasting is evil. (James 4:13–16)

Spiritual Insight

Pause to ask that the Holy Spirit would give you understanding and insight into the word of truth, so that you will have a growing grasp of your identity in Christ—where you came from, who you are, and where you are going. Ask for a clearer understanding of God's purpose for your life.

31

Concerns for Others

May I not be selfish, not live to make a good impression on others. May I be humble, thinking of others as better than myself and not thinking only about my own affairs. May I be interested in others, too, and what they are doing. (Philippians 2:3–4)

Other Believers

Intercede in the lives of your personal friends, and ask that the Lord will bless their families, their careers, and their ministries. Pray that he will comfort and strengthen those who are oppressed and in need.

Prayer of Thanksgiving

I still belong to you; you are holding my right hand. You will keep on guiding me with your counsel, leading me to a glorious destiny. (Psalm 73:23–24)

Pause to offer your own expressions of thanksgiving.

Concluding Prayer

May God, who gives patience and encouragement, help me live in complete harmony with others—with the attitude of Christ Jesus toward others. Then we can all join together with one voice, giving praise and glory to God, the Father of our Lord Jesus Christ. (Romans 15:5–6)

Now may the God of peace make us holy in every way, and may our whole spirit and soul and body be kept blameless until that day when our Lord Jesus Christ comes again. God, who calls us, is faithful; he will do this. (1 Thessalonians 5:23–24)

Day 8

Praise and Worship

Great is the LORD! He is most worthy of praise! He is to be revered above all gods. The gods of other nations are merely idols, but the LORD made the heavens! Honor and majesty surround him; strength and beauty are in his dwelling. O nations of the world, recognize the LORD, recognize that the LORD is glorious and strong. Give to the LORD the glory he deserves! Bring your offering and come to worship him. Worship the LORD in all his holy splendor. Let all the earth tremble before him. The world is firmly established and cannot be shaken. (1 Chronicles 16:25–30)

You are the God of Abraham and the awe-inspiring God of Isaac. (Genesis 31:42)

Pause to express your thoughts of praise and worship.

Personal Examination

How can I know all the sins lurking in my heart? Cleanse me from these hidden faults. Keep me from deliberate sins! Don't let them control me. Then I will be free of guilt and innocent of great sin. (Psalm 19:12–13)

Ask the Spirit to search your heart and reveal any areas of unconfessed sin. Acknowledge these to the Lord and thank him for his forgiveness.

Commitment

May I take care not to do my good deeds publicly, to be admired, because then I will lose the reward from my Father in heaven. (Matthew 6:1)

May I not be afraid of those who want to kill me. They can only kill my body; they cannot touch my soul. May I fear only you, who can destroy both soul and body in hell. (Matthew 10:28)

Pause to add your own prayers for commitment and renewal.

Personal Concerns

By God's grace I want to live to the end in faith, knowing that I will not receive what is promised on earth, but seeing from a distance and welcoming the promises of God. I agree that I am no more than a foreigner and nomad here on earth. But I am looking for a better place, a heavenly homeland. That is why God is not ashamed to be called my God, for he has prepared a heavenly city for me. Like Moses, may I consider it better to suffer for the sake of the Messiah than to own treasures, for I am looking ahead to the great reward that God will give me. (Hebrews 11:13, 16, 26)

Love and Compassion

Pause to ask for the grace of greater love and compassion for others. Pray that you will become a more Christlike person who considers the needs of others above your own, knowing that God is your provider and sustainer.

Concerns for Others

All this newness of life is from God, who brought us back to himself through what Christ did. And God has given us the task of reconciling people to him. For God was in Christ, reconciling the world to himself, no longer counting people's sins against them. This is the wonderful message he has given us to tell others. We are Christ's ambassadors, and God is using us to speak to you. We urge you, as though Christ himself were here pleading with you, "Be reconciled to God!" (2 Corinthians 5:18–20)

Christian Witness

Pray on behalf of the people you personally know who have not yet entered into the joy of a personal relationship with Jesus. Intercede for your unsaved relatives, neighbors, co-workers, and friends.

Prayer of Thanksgiving

It is God who gives me the ability to stand firm for Christ. He has commissioned me, and he has identified me as his own by placing the Holy Spirit in my heart as the first installment of everything he will give me. (2 Corinthians 1:21–22)

Thanks be to God, who made us his captives and leads us along in Christ's triumphal procession. Now wherever we go he uses us to tell others about the Lord and to spread the Good News like a sweet perfume. (2 Corinthians 2:14)

Pause to offer your own expressions of thanksgiving.

35

Concluding Prayer

The LORD is my shepherd; I have everything I need. He lets me rest in green meadows; he leads me beside peaceful streams. He renews my strength. He guides me along right paths, bringing honor to his name. Even when I walk through the dark valley of death, I will not be afraid, for you are close beside me. Your rod and your staff protect and comfort me. You prepare a feast for me in the presence of my enemies. You welcome me as a guest, anointing my head with oil. My cup overflows with blessings. Surely your goodness and unfailing love will pursue me all the days of my life, and I will live in the house of the LORD forever. (Psalm 23:1–6)

Day 9

Praise and Worship

In the year King Uzziah died, I saw the LORD. He was sitting on a lofty throne, and the train of his robe filled the Temple. Hovering around him were mighty seraphim, each with six wings. With two wings they covered their faces, with two they covered their feet, and with the remaining two they flew. In a great chorus they sang, "Holy, holy, holy is the LORD Almighty! The whole earth is filled with his glory!" (Isaiah 6:1–3)

The Lord God is the Alpha and the Omega—the beginning and the end, the one who is, who always was, and who is still to come, the Almighty One. (Revelation 1:8)

Pause to express your thoughts of praise and worship.

Personal Examination

The Sovereign LORD, the Holy One of Israel, says, "Only in returning to me and waiting for me will you be saved. In quietness and confidence is your strength." (Isaiah 30:15)

Ask the Spirit to search your heart and reveal any areas of unconfessed sin. Acknowledge these to the Lord and thank him for his forgiveness.

Commitment

May I not use foul or abusive language. May everything I say be good and helpful, so that my words will be an encouragement to those who hear them. (Ephesians 4:29)

I have been born again. My new life did not come from my earthly parents because the life they gave me will end in death. But this new life will last forever because it comes from the eternal, living word of God. So may I get rid of all malicious behavior and deceit. May I not just pretend to be good, but be done with hypocrisy and jealousy and backstabbing! (1 Peter 1:23; 2:1)

Pause to add your own prayers for commitment and renewal.

Personal Concerns

May I not be afraid, because the Lord Jesus is here. (Mark 6:50)

Faithfulness as a Steward
Pause to ask that God would empower you to become a more faithful and effective steward with all that he has entrusted to your care. Since he has given you a stewardship of talents, treasure, truth, time, and love and compassion, ask that you would use these gifts with fidelity in his service.

Concerns for Others

It is God's will that your good lives should silence those who make foolish accusations against you. You are not slaves; you are free. But your freedom is not an excuse to do evil. You are free to live as God's slaves. Show respect for everyone. Love your Christian brothers and sisters. Fear God. Show respect for the king. (1 Peter 2:15–17)

Government

Lift up those in local, state, and national government, and pray that those in positions of authority would look to God for wisdom in their decisions and practice.

Prayer of Thanksgiving

Once I was far away from God. I was his enemy, separated from him by my evil thoughts and actions, yet now he has brought me back as his friend. He has done this through his death on the cross in his own human body. As a result, he has brought me into the very presence of God, and I am holy and blameless as I stand before him without a single fault. (Colossians 1:21–22)

Pause to offer your own expressions of thanksgiving.

Concluding Prayer

I love you, LORD; you are my strength. The LORD is my rock, my fortress, and my savior; my God is my rock, in whom I find protection. He is my shield, the strength of my salvation, and my stronghold. I will call on the LORD, who is worthy of praise, for he saves me from my enemies. (Psalm 18:1–3)

Many sorrows come to the wicked, but unfailing love surrounds those who trust the LORD. (Psalm 32:10)

Day 10

Praise and Worship

O LORD, you have examined my heart and know everything about me. You know when I sit down or stand up. You know my every thought when far away. You chart the path ahead of me and tell me where to stop and rest. Every moment you know where I am. You know what I am going to say even before I say it, LORD. You both precede and follow me. You place your hand of blessing on my head. Such knowledge is too wonderful for me, too great for me to know! (Psalm 139:1–6)

Pause to express your thoughts of praise and worship.

Personal Examination

May I return to the LORD my God, for my sins have brought me down. May I bring my petitions, and return to the LORD. I will say to him, "Forgive all my sins and graciously receive me, so that I may offer you the sacrifice of praise." (Hosea 14:1–2)

Ask the Spirit to search your heart and reveal any areas of unconfessed sin. Acknowledge these to the Lord and thank him for his forgiveness.

Commitment

May I not be like the rocky soil that represents those who hear the message and receive it with joy but like young plants in such soil, their roots don't go very deep. At first they get along fine, but they wilt as soon as they have problems or are persecuted because they believe the word. And may I not be like the thorny ground which represents those who hear and accept the Good News, but all too quickly the message is crowded out by the cares of this life and the lure of wealth, so no crop is produced. Instead, may I be like the good soil which represents the hearts of those who truly accept God's message and produce a huge harvest—thirty, sixty, or even a hundred times as much as had been planted. (Matthew 13:20–23; Mark 4:16–20; Luke 8:13–15)

Pause to add your own prayers for commitment and renewal.

Personal Concerns

Since I am surrounded by such a huge crowd of witnesses to the life of faith, let me strip off every weight that slows me down, especially the sin that so easily hinders my progress. And let me run with endurance the race that God has set before me. May I do this by keeping my eyes on Jesus, on whom my faith depends from start to finish. He was willing to die a shameful death on the cross because of the joy he knew would be his afterward. Now he is seated in the place of highest honor beside God's throne in heaven. I will think about all he endured when sinful people did such terrible things to him, so that I don't become weary and give up. (Hebrews 12:1–3)

Family and Ministry

Pause to lift up your family, your career, and your ministry before the Lord. Ask that you would have the privilege of sharing Christ with others and helping people grow in their knowledge of him.

Concerns for Others

The Spirit of the Lord is upon me, for he has appointed me to preach Good News to the poor. He has sent me to proclaim that captives will be released, that the blind will see, that the downtrodden will be freed from their oppressors, and that the time of the Lord's favor has come. (Luke 4:18–19)

Missions

Intercede for national and world missions, and pray that those who have dedicated their lives to the fulfillment of the Great Commission will be strengthened, encouraged, and empowered.

Prayer of Thanksgiving

We should know about what will happen to the Christians who have died so we will not be full of sorrow like people who have no hope. For since we believe that Jesus died and was raised to life again, we also believe that when Jesus comes, God will bring back with Jesus all the Christians who have died. According to the Lord, we who are still living when he returns will not rise to meet him ahead of those who are in their graves. For the Lord himself will come down from heaven with a commanding shout, with the call of the archangel, and with the trumpet call of God.

First, all the Christians who have died will rise from their graves. Then, together with them, we who are still alive and remain on the earth will be caught up in the clouds to meet the Lord in the air and remain with him forever. (1 Thessalonians 4:13–17)

Pause to offer your own expressions of thanksgiving.

Concluding Prayer

The LORD is God, and he created the heavens and earth and put everything in place. He made the world to be lived in, not to be a place of empty chaos. He is the LORD, and there is no other. (Isaiah 45:18)

The LORD is in his holy Temple. Let all the earth be silent before him. (Habakkuk 2:20)

Day 11

Praise and Worship

After this I saw a vast crowd, too great to count, from every nation and tribe and people and language, standing in front of the throne and before the Lamb. They were clothed in white and held palm branches in their hands. And they were shouting with a mighty shout, "Salvation comes from our God on the throne and from the Lamb!" (Revelation 7:9–10)

Bless the King who comes in the name of the Lord! Peace in heaven and glory in highest heaven! (Luke 19:38)

Pause to express your thoughts of praise and worship.

Personal Examination

You spread out our sins before you—our secret sins—and you see them all. (Psalm 90:8)

Ask the Spirit to search your heart and reveal any areas of unconfessed sin. Acknowledge these to the Lord and thank him for his forgiveness.

Commitment

Like Enoch, may I enjoy a close relationship with God throughout my life. (Genesis 5:24)

Like Noah, may I find favor with the LORD. (Genesis 6:8)

Pause to add your own prayers for commitment and renewal.

Personal Concerns

May I put to death the sinful, earthly things lurking within me, and may I have nothing to do with sexual sin, impurity, lust, and shameful desires. May I not be greedy for the good things of this life, for that is idolatry. God's terrible anger will come upon those who do such things. I used to do them when my life was still part of this world. (Colossians 3:5–7)

Growth in Character
Pause to look to the Lord for the power to stand firm in the spiritual warfare against the world, the flesh, and spiritual forces of wickedness. Ask that you would grow in character and pursue the disciplines of the faith in a spirit of radical dependence upon him.

Concerns for Others

The end of the world is coming soon. Therefore, be earnest and disciplined in your prayers. (1 Peter 4:7)

World Affairs
Lift up the needs of the poor and the hungry, the oppressed and the persecuted. Pray for those in positions of authority and ask for the blessings of peace rather than conflict.

Prayer of Thanksgiving

I look forward to that wonderful event when the glory of my great God and Savior, Jesus Christ, will be revealed. He gave his life to free us from every kind of sin, to cleanse us, and to make us his very own people, totally committed to doing what is right. (Titus 2:13–14)

The Lord will deliver me from every evil attack and will bring me safely to his heavenly Kingdom. To God be the glory forever and ever. Amen. (2 Timothy 4:18)

Pause to offer your own expressions of thanksgiving.

Concluding Prayer

Come and listen, all you who fear God, and I will tell you what he did for me. For I cried out to him for help, praising him as I spoke. If I had not confessed the sin in my heart, my LORD would not have listened. But God did listen! He paid attention to my prayer. Praise God, who did not ignore my prayer and did not withdraw his unfailing love from me. (Psalm 66:16–20)

Day 12

Praise and Worship

Praise the LORD! Yes, give praise, O servants of the LORD. Praise the name of the LORD! Blessed be the name of the LORD forever and ever. Everywhere—from east to west—praise the name of the LORD. For the LORD is high above the nations; his glory is far greater than the heavens. Who can be compared with the LORD our God, who is enthroned on high? Far below him are the heavens and the earth. He stoops to look. (Psalm 113:1–6)

Pause to express your thoughts of praise and worship.

Personal Examination

But I confess my sins; I am deeply sorry for what I have done. Do not abandon me, LORD. Do not stand at a distance, my God. Come quickly to help me, O LORD my savior. I confess my iniquity. (Psalm 38:18, 21–22)

Ask the Spirit to search your heart and reveal any areas of unconfessed sin. Acknowledge these to the Lord and thank him for his forgiveness.

Commitment

May I listen to you and treasure your instructions, tune my ears to wisdom, and concentrate on understanding. May I cry out for insight and understanding. I will search for you as I would for lost money or hidden trea-

sure. Then I will understand what it means to fear the
LORD, and I will gain knowledge of God. Then I will
understand what is right, just, and fair, I will know how
to find the right course of action every time. For wisdom
will enter my heart, and knowledge will fill me with
joy. Wise planning will watch over me. Understanding
will keep me safe. (Proverbs 2:1–5, 9–11)

Pause to add your own prayers for commitment and renewal.

Personal Concerns

May I not love this evil world and all that it offers me,
for when I love the world, I show that I do not have
the love of the Father in me. For the world offers only
the lust for physical pleasure, the lust for everything we
see, and pride in our possessions. These are not from
the Father. They are from this evil world. And this
world is fading away, along with everything it craves.
But if you do the will of God, you will live forever.
(1 John 2:15–17)

Knowing, Loving, and Trusting God
*Pause to ask God for the grace to know and please him. Ask
him to enlarge your capacity to love him more and abide
wholly in him.*

Concerns for Others

There is no longer Jew or Gentile, slave or free, male
or female. For you are all Christians—we are one in
Christ Jesus. (Galatians 3:28)

Churches and Ministries

Ask God to work on behalf of the people and concerns at your local church. Pray for his blessing and power in the ministries that are engaged in Christian witness, discipleship, education, and those serving people in need.

Prayer of Thanksgiving

God paid a ransom to save me from the empty life I inherited from my ancestors. And the ransom he paid was not mere gold or silver. He paid for me with the precious lifeblood of Christ, the sinless, spotless Lamb of God. (1 Peter 1:18–19)

See how very much our heavenly Father loves us, for he allows us to be called his children, and we really are! But the people who belong to this world don't know God, so they don't understand that we are his. (1 John 3:1)

Pause to offer your own expressions of thanksgiving.

Concluding Prayer

All of your works will thank you, LORD, and your faithful followers will bless you. They will talk together about the glory of your kingdom; they will celebrate examples of your power. They will tell about your mighty deeds and about the majesty and glory of your reign. For your kingdom is an everlasting kingdom. You rule generation after generation. You are faithful in all you say; you are gracious in all you do. (Psalm 145:10–13)

Be exalted, O God, above the highest heavens. May your glory shine over all the earth. (Psalm 108:5)

Day 13

Praise and Worship

The Son reflects God's own glory, and everything about him represents God exactly. He sustains the universe by the mighty power of his command. After he died to cleanse us from the stain of sin, he sat down in the place of honor at the right hand of the majestic God of heaven. (Hebrews 1:3–4)

Pause to express your thoughts of praise and worship.

Personal Examination

But you desire honesty from the heart, so you can teach me to be wise in my inmost being. (Psalm 51:6)

Ask the Spirit to search your heart and reveal any areas of unconfessed sin. Acknowledge these to the Lord and thank him for his forgiveness.

Commitment

The heavenly Father to whom we pray has no favorites when he judges. He will judge or reward us according to what we do. So we must live in reverent fear of him during our time as foreigners here on earth. (1 Peter 1:17)

May I obey the commands of the LORD my God by walking in your ways and fearing you, serving only you and fearing you alone. May I obey your commands, listen to your voice, and cling to you. (Deuteronomy 8:6; 13:4)

Pause to add your own prayers for commitment and renewal.

Personal Concerns

No one who trusts in you will ever be disgraced, but disgrace comes to those who try to deceive others. Show me the path where I should walk, O Lord; point out the right road for me to follow. Lead me by your truth and teach me, for you are the God who saves me. All day long I put my hope in you. (Psalm 25:3–5)

Greater Wisdom

Pause to ask God for the grace to develop an eternal perspective on your life and concerns, and that he would renew your mind with his truth. Ask for the power to order your steps with wisdom and skill in each area of life so that you will seek to please him rather than impress others.

Concerns for Others

May my love for others overflow more and more, and may I keep on growing in my knowledge and understanding. For I want to understand what really matters, so that I may live a pure and blameless life until Christ returns. May I always be filled with the fruit of my salvation—those good things that are produced in my life by Jesus Christ—for this will bring much glory and praise to God. (Philippians 1:9–11)

Loved Ones

*Lift up the members of your immediate family and your
extended family. Pray for the spiritual, emotional, and
physical concerns of your loved ones.*

Prayer of Thanksgiving

I give thanks to the LORD, for he is good! His faithful
love endures forever. (1 Chronicles 16:34)

But in my distress I cried out to the LORD; yes, I prayed
to my God for help. He heard me from his sanctuary; my cry reached his ears. He led me to a place of
safety; he rescued me because he delights in me. (Psalm
18:6, 19)

Pause to offer your own expressions of thanksgiving.

Concluding Prayer

Happy are those who hear the joyful call to worship,
for they will walk in the light of your presence, LORD.
They rejoice all day long in your wonderful reputation.
They exult in your righteousness. (Psalm 89:15–16)

Day 14

Praise and Worship

O Lord, God of our ancestors, you alone are the God who is in heaven. You are ruler of all the kingdoms of the earth. You are powerful and mighty; no one can stand against you! (2 Chronicles 20:6)

I will thank you, Lord, with all my heart; I will tell of all the marvelous things you have done. I will be filled with joy because of you. I will sing praises to your name, O Most High. (Psalm 9:1–2)

Pause to express your thoughts of praise and worship.

Personal Examination

The Lord is watching everywhere, keeping his eye on both the evil and the good. (Proverbs 15:3)

Ask the Spirit to search your heart and reveal any areas of unconfessed sin. Acknowledge these to the Lord and thank him for his forgiveness.

Commitment

May I not be troubled. Let me trust God and Christ. (John 14:1)

You have loved me even as the Father has loved you. May I remain in your love. When I obey you, I remain in your love, just as you obey your Father and remain in his love. (John 15:9–11)

God forbid that I should boast about anything except the cross of our Lord Jesus Christ. Because of that cross, my interest in this world died long ago, and the world's interest in me is also long dead. (Galatians 6:14)

Pause to add your own prayers for commitment and renewal.

Personal Concerns

Stop loving this evil world and all that it offers you, for when you love the world, you show that you do not have the love of the Father in you. For the world offers only the lust for physical pleasure, the lust for everything we see, and pride in our possessions. These are not from the Father. They are from this evil world. And this world is fading away, along with everything it craves. But if you do the will of God, you will live forever. (1 John 2:15–17)

Spiritual Insight
Pause to ask that the Holy Spirit would give you understanding and insight into the word of truth, so that you will have a growing grasp of your identity in Christ—where you came from, who you are, and where you are going. Ask for a clearer understanding of God's purpose for your life.

Concerns for Others

Pure and lasting religion in the sight of God our Father means that we must care for orphans and widows in their troubles, and refuse to let the world corrupt us. (James 1:27)

Other Believers

Intercede in the lives of your personal friends, and ask that the Lord will bless their families, their careers, and their ministries. Pray that he will comfort and strengthen those who are oppressed and in need.

Prayer of Thanksgiving

God made Christ, who never sinned, to be the offering for our sin, so that we could be made right with God through Christ. (2 Corinthians 5:21)

Long ago, even before he made the world, God loved me and chose me in Christ to be holy and without fault in his eyes. His unchanging plan has always been to adopt me into his own family by bringing me to himself through Jesus Christ. And this gave him great pleasure. So I praise God for the wonderful kindness he has poured out on me because I belong to his dearly loved Son. (Ephesians 1:4–6)

Pause to offer your own expressions of thanksgiving.

Concluding Prayer

I will enter his gates with thanksgiving; go into his courts with praise. I will give thanks to him and bless his name. For the LORD is good. His unfailing love continues forever, and his faithfulness continues to each generation. (Psalm 100:4–5)

May the glory of the LORD last forever! The LORD rejoices in all he has made! (Psalm 104:31)

Day 15

Praise and Worship

Praise the LORD! Praise God in his heavenly dwelling; praise him in his mighty heaven! Praise him for his mighty works; praise his unequaled greatness! Praise him with a blast of the trumpet; praise him with the lyre and harp! Praise him with the tambourine and dancing; praise him with stringed instruments and flutes! Praise him with a clash of cymbals; praise him with loud clanging cymbals. Let everything that lives sing praises to the LORD! Praise the LORD! (Psalm 150:1–6)

The LORD will reign forever and ever! (Exodus 15:18)

Pause to express your thoughts of praise and worship.

Personal Examination

Where is another God like you, who pardons the sins of the survivors among his people? You cannot stay angry with your people forever, because you delight in showing mercy. Once again you will have compassion on us. You will trample our sins under your feet and throw them into the depths of the ocean! (Micah 7:18–19)

Ask the Spirit to search your heart and reveal any areas of unconfessed sin. Acknowledge these to the Lord and thank him for his forgiveness.

Commitment

I will not let sin control the way I live and not give in to its lustful desires. I will not let any part of my body become a tool of wickedness, to be used for sinning. Instead, I give myself completely to God since I have been given new life. And I use my whole body as a tool to do what is right for the glory of God. (Romans 6:12–13)

May I get rid of all the filth and evil in my life, and humbly accept the message God has planted in my heart, for it is strong enough to save my soul. (James 1:21)

Pause to add your own prayers for commitment and renewal.

Personal Concerns

Answer me when I call, O God who declares me innocent. Take away my distress. Have mercy on me and hear my prayer. (Psalm 4:1)

Knowing, Loving, and Trusting God
Pause to ask God for the grace to know and please him. Ask him to enlarge your capacity to love him more and abide wholly in him.

Concerns for Others

Believe in the LORD your God, and you will be able to stand firm. Believe in his prophets, and you will succeed. (2 Chronicles 20:20)

Churches and Ministries

*Ask God to work on behalf of the people and concerns at your
local church. Pray for his blessing and power in the ministries
that are engaged in Christian witness, discipleship, education,
and those serving people in need.*

Prayer of Thanksgiving

I will sing about your power. I will shout with joy each
morning because of your unfailing love. For you have
been my refuge, a place of safety in the day of distress.
O my Strength, to you I sing praises, for you, O God,
are my refuge, the God who shows me unfailing love.
(Psalm 59:16–17)

Pause to offer your own expressions of thanksgiving.

Concluding Prayer

May the grace of our Lord Jesus Christ, the love of
God, and the fellowship of the Holy Spirit be with us.
(2 Corinthians 13:13)

Blessed be the Lord forever! Amen and Amen. (Psalm
89:52)

Day 16

Praise and Worship

The Son of Man will come with the clouds of heaven. He will approach the Ancient One and be led into his presence. He will be given authority, honor, and royal power over all the nations of the world, so that people of every race and nation and language will obey him. His rule is eternal—it will never end. His kingdom will never be destroyed. (Daniel 7:13–14)

Jesus is my Lord and my God! (John 20:28)

Pause to express your thoughts of praise and worship.

Personal Examination

Oh, my LORD! Please don't punish us for this sin we have so foolishly committed. (Numbers 12:11)

Ask the Spirit to search your heart and reveal any areas of unconfessed sin. Acknowledge these to the Lord and thank him for his forgiveness.

Commitment

May I not have self-confidence while I scorn everyone else. (Luke 18:9)

May I not be like those who do not trust in God. They trust their wealth instead and grow more and more bold in their wickedness. (Psalm 52:7)

Pause to add your own prayers for commitment and renewal.

Personal Concerns

May I not throw away this confident trust in the Lord, no matter what happens. May I remember the great reward it brings me! Patient endurance is what I need now, so I will continue to do God's will. Then I will receive all that he has promised. (Hebrews 10:35–36)

Greater Wisdom

Pause to ask God for the grace to develop an eternal perspective on your life and concerns, and that he would renew your mind with his truth. Ask for the power to order your steps with wisdom and skill in each area of life so that you will seek to please him rather than impress others.

Concerns for Others

Don't think only of your own good. Think of other Christians and what is best for them. (1 Corinthians 10:24)

Loved Ones

Lift up the members of your immediate family and your extended family. Pray for the spiritual, emotional, and physical concerns of your loved ones.

Prayer of Thanksgiving

I will declare the wonder of your name to my brothers and sisters. I will praise you among all your people. Praise the LORD, all you who fear him! Honor him, all you descendants of Jacob! Show him reverence, all you descendants of Israel! For he has not ignored the suffering of the needy. He has not turned and walked away. He has listened to their cries for help. (Psalm 22:22–24)

Pause to offer your own expressions of thanksgiving.

Concluding Prayer

God is able to make us strong, just as the Good News says. It is the message about Jesus Christ and his plan for us Gentiles, a plan kept secret from the beginning of time. But now as the prophets foretold and as the eternal God has commanded, this message is made known to all Gentiles everywhere, so that they might believe and obey Christ. To God, who alone is wise, be the glory forever through Jesus Christ. Amen. (Romans 16:25–27)

Day 17

Praise and Worship

The earth is the LORD's, and everything in it. The world and all its people belong to him. For he laid the earth's foundation on the seas and built it on the ocean depths. (Psalm 24:1–2)

It is God who sits above the circle of the earth. The people below must seem to him like grasshoppers! He is the one who spreads out the heavens like a curtain and makes his tent from them. He judges the great people of the world and brings them all to nothing. (Isaiah 40:22–23)

Pause to express your thoughts of praise and worship.

Personal Examination

Turn to me now, while there is time! Give me your hearts. Come with fasting, weeping, and mourning. Don't tear your clothing in your grief; instead, tear your hearts. Return to the LORD your God, for he is gracious and merciful. He is not easily angered. He is filled with kindness and is eager not to punish you. (Joel 2:12–13)

Ask the Spirit to search your heart and reveal any areas of unconfessed sin. Acknowledge these to the Lord and thank him for his forgiveness.

Commitment

Like Josiah, may I do what is pleasing in the LORD's sight and follow the example of David, not turning aside from doing what is right. May I turn to the LORD with all my heart and soul and strength, obeying all of your word. (2 Kings 22:1–2; 23:25)

These are the things that I must do: tell the truth to others, render judgments that are just and that lead to peace, make no evil plots to harm others and stop the habit of swearing to things that are false. The LORD hates all these things. (Zechariah 8:16–17)

Pause to add your own prayers for commitment and renewal.

Personal Concerns

May I not weary myself trying to get rich. Why waste my time? Riches can disappear as though they had the wings of a bird! (Proverbs 23:4–5)

Spiritual Insight

Pause to ask that the Holy Spirit would give you understanding and insight into the word of truth, so that you will have a growing grasp of your identity in Christ—where you came from, who you are, and where you are going. Ask for a clearer understanding of God's purpose for your life.

Concerns for Others

It is possible to give freely and become more wealthy, but those who are stingy will lose everything. The generous prosper and are satisfied; those who refresh others will themselves be refreshed. (Proverbs 11:24)

Other Believers

Intercede in the lives of your personal friends, and ask that the Lord will bless their families, their careers, and their ministries. Pray that he will comfort and strengthen those who are oppressed and in need.

Prayer of Thanksgiving

You who love the Lord, hate evil! He protects the lives of his godly people and rescues them from the power of the wicked. Light shines on the godly, and joy on those who do right. (Psalm 97:10–11)

Pause to offer your own expressions of thanksgiving.

Concluding Prayer

Lord, there is no one like you! For you are great, and your name is full of power. Who would not fear you, O King of nations? That title belongs to you alone! Among all the wise people of the earth and in all the kingdoms of the world, there is no one like you. (Jeremiah 10:6–7)

Our Father in heaven, may your name be honored. May your Kingdom come soon. May your will be done here on earth, just as it is in heaven. (Matthew 6:9–10)

Day 18

Praise and Worship

Who put the world in his care? Who has set the whole world in place? If God were to take back his spirit and withdraw his breath, all life would cease, and humanity would turn again to dust. (Job 34:13–15)

For all the animals of the forest are yours, and you own the cattle on a thousand hills. Every bird of the mountains and all the animals of the field belong to you. (Psalm 50:10–11)

Pause to express your thoughts of praise and worship.

Personal Examination

If I say I have no sin, I am only fooling myself and refusing to accept the truth. But if I confess my sins to him, he is faithful and just to forgive me and to cleanse me from every wrong. If I claim I have not sinned, I am calling God a liar and showing that his word has no place in my heart. (1 John 1:8–10)

Ask the Spirit to search your heart and reveal any areas of unconfessed sin. Acknowledge these to the Lord and thank him for his forgiveness.

Commitment

May I not get tired of doing what is good and not get discouraged and give up, for we will reap a harvest of blessing at the appropriate time. (Galatians 6:9)

May I not bring sorrow to God's Holy Spirit by whom I will be saved on the day of redemption. (Ephesians 4:30)

May I be careful to put into action God's saving work in my life, obeying God with deep reverence and fear. For God is working in me, giving me the desire to obey him and the power to do what pleases him. (Philippians 2:12–13)

Pause to add your own prayers for commitment and renewal.

Personal Concerns

Protect me! Rescue my life from my enemies! Do not let me be disgraced, for I trust in you. May integrity and honesty protect me, for I put my hope in you. (Psalm 25:20–21)

Love and Compassion

Pause to ask for the grace of greater love and compassion for others. Pray that you will become a more Christlike person who considers the needs of others above your own, knowing that God is your provider and sustainer.

Concerns for Others

Just as our bodies have many parts and each part has a special function, so it is with Christ's body. We are all parts of his one body, and each of us has different work to do. And since we are all one body in Christ, we belong to each other, and each of us needs all the others. God has given each of us the ability to do certain things well. So if God has given you the ability to prophesy, speak out when you have faith that God is speaking through you. (Romans 12:4–6)

Christian Witness

Pray on behalf of the people you personally know who have not yet entered into the joy of a personal relationship with Jesus. Intercede for your unsaved relatives, neighbors, co-workers, and friends.

Prayer of Thanksgiving

"Don't be afraid!" he said. "I bring you good news of great joy for everyone! The Savior—yes, the Messiah, the Lord—has been born tonight in Bethlehem, the city of David!" (Luke 2:10–11)

The Son of Man came to seek and to save those who are lost. (Luke 19:10)

To all who believed him and accepted him, he gave the right to become children of God. They are reborn! This is not a physical birth resulting from human passion or plan—this rebirth comes from God. (John 1:12–13)

Pause to offer your own expressions of thanksgiving.

Concluding Prayer

God showed how much he loved us by sending his only Son into the world so that we might have eternal life through him. This is real love. It is not that we loved God, but that he loved us and sent his Son as a sacrifice to take away our sins. (1 John 4:9–10)

Love is patient and kind. Love is not jealous or boastful or proud or rude. Love does not demand its own way. Love is not irritable, and it keeps no record of when it has been wronged. It is never glad about injustice but rejoices whenever the truth wins out. Love never gives up, never loses faith, is always hopeful, and endures through every circumstance. Love will last forever, but prophecy and speaking in unknown languages and special knowledge will all disappear. (1 Corinthians 13:4–8)

Day 19

Praise and Worship

The LORD gives righteousness and justice to all who are treated unfairly. The LORD is merciful and gracious; he is slow to get angry and full of unfailing love. (Psalm 103:6, 8)

Your throne is founded on two strong pillars—righteousness and justice. Unfailing love and truth walk before you as attendants. (Psalm 89:14)

Pause to express your thoughts of praise and worship.

Personal Examination

O LORD, have mercy on me; Heal me, for I have sinned against you. (Psalm 41:4)

Ask the Spirit to search your heart and reveal any areas of unconfessed sin. Acknowledge these to the Lord and thank him for his forgiveness.

Commitment

May I guard my heart, For it affects everything I do. (Proverbs 4:23)

May I not worry about tomorrow, for tomorrow will bring its own worries. Today's trouble is enough for today. (Matthew 6:34)

May I be ready all the time, for the Son of Man will come when least expected. (Matthew 24:44; Luke 12:40)

Pause to add your own prayers for commitment and renewal.

Personal Concerns

God is the one who gives seed to the farmer and then bread to eat. In the same way, he will give you many opportunities to do good, and he will produce a great harvest of generosity in you. Yes, you will be enriched so that you can give even more generously. And when we take your gifts to those who need them, they will break out in thanksgiving to God. So two good things will happen—the needs of the Christians in Jerusalem will be met, and they will joyfully express their thanksgiving to God. You will be glorifying God through your generous gifts. For your generosity to them will prove that you are obedient to the Good News of Christ. And they will pray for you with deep affection because of the wonderful grace of God shown through you. Thank God for his Son—a gift too wonderful for words! (2 Corinthians 9:10–15)

Faithfulness as a Steward

Pause to ask that God would empower you to become a more faithful and effective steward with all that he has entrusted to your care. Since he has given you a stewardship of talents, treasure, truth, time, and love and compassion, ask that you would use these gifts with fidelity in his service.

Concerns for Others

Honor the LORD with your wealth and with the best part of everything your land produces. Then he will fill your barns with grain, and your vats will overflow with the finest wine. (Proverbs 3:9–10)

Government

Lift up those in local, state, and national government, and pray that those in positions of authority would look to God for wisdom in their decisions and practice.

Prayer of Thanksgiving

LORD, you were oppressed and treated harshly, yet you never said a word. You were led as a lamb to the slaughter. And as a sheep is silent before the shearers, you did not open your mouth. From prison and trial they led you away to your death. But who among the people realized that you were dying for their sins—that you were suffering their punishment? You had done no wrong, and you never deceived anyone. But you were buried like a criminal; you were put in a rich man's grave. But it was the LORD's good plan to crush you and fill you with grief. Yet when your life is made an offering for sin, you will have a multitude of children, many heirs. You will enjoy a long life, and the LORD's plan will prosper in your hands. When you see all that is accomplished by your anguish, you will be satisfied. And because of what you have experienced, God's righteous servant, God will make it possible for many to be counted righteous, for you will bear all their sins. God will give you the honors of one who is mighty and great, because you exposed yourself to death. You were counted among those who were sinners. You bore the sins of many and interceded for sinners. (Isaiah 53:7–12)

Pause to offer your own expressions of thanksgiving.

Concluding Prayer

I will keep on hoping for you to help me; I will praise you more and more. I will tell everyone about your righteousness. All day long I will proclaim your saving power, for I am overwhelmed by how much you have done for me. I will praise your mighty deeds, O Sovereign LORD. I will tell everyone that you alone are just and good. O God, you have taught me from my earliest childhood, and I have constantly told others about the wonderful things you do. (Psalm 71:14–17)

I will lie down in peace and sleep, for you alone, O LORD, will keep me safe. (Psalm 4:8)

Day 20

Praise and Worship

Praise the Lord! Praise the Lord, I tell myself. I will praise the Lord as long as I live. I will sing praises to my God even with my dying breath. (Psalm 146:1–2)

I will praise the Lord, and everyone on earth will bless his holy name forever and forever. (Psalm 145:21)

Pause to express your thoughts of praise and worship.

Personal Examination

He sees everything I do and every step I take. (Job 31:4)

Ask the Spirit to search your heart and reveal any areas of unconfessed sin. Acknowledge these to the Lord and thank him for his forgiveness.

Commitment

May I not worship any other gods besides you. (Exodus 20:3; Deuteronomy 5:7)

May I not make idols of any kind. (Exodus 20:4; Deuteronomy 5:8)

May I not misuse the name of the Lord my God. The Lord will not let anyone go unpunished who misuses his name. (Exodus 20:7; Deuteronomy 5:11)

Pause to add your own prayers for commitment and renewal.

Personal Concerns

Give us our food for today, and forgive us our sins, just as we have forgiven those who have sinned against us. And don't let us yield to temptation, but deliver us from the evil one. (Matthew 6:11–13)

Family and Ministry

Pause to lift up your family, your career, and your ministry before the Lord. Ask that you would have the privilege of sharing Christ with others and helping people grow in their knowledge of him.

Concerns for Others

May I not get tired of doing what is good and not get discouraged and give up, for we will reap a harvest of blessing at the appropriate time. Whenever I have the opportunity, may I do good to everyone, especially to my Christian brothers and sisters. (Galatians 6:9–10)

Missions

Intercede for national and world missions, and pray that those who have dedicated their lives to the fulfillment of the Great Commission will be strengthened, encouraged, and empowered.

Prayer of Thanksgiving

Praise the Lord, the God of Israel, because he has visited his people and redeemed them. He has sent us a mighty Savior from the royal line of his servant David, just as he promised through his holy prophets long ago. Now we will be saved from our enemies and from all who hate us. He has been merciful to our ancestors by remembering his sacred covenant with them, the covenant he gave to our ancestor Abraham. We have been rescued from our enemies, so we can serve God without fear, in holiness and righteousness forever. (Luke 1:68–75)

Pause to offer your own expressions of thanksgiving.

Concluding Prayer

The LORD grants wisdom! From his mouth come knowledge and understanding. He grants a treasure of good sense to the godly. He is their shield, protecting those who walk with integrity. He guards the paths of justice and protects those who are faithful to him. (Proverbs 2:6–8)

Day 21

Praise and Worship

Those who are wise will take all this to heart; they will see in our history the faithful love of the LORD. (Psalm 107:43)

All your words are true; all your just laws will stand forever. (Psalm 119:160)

You are the God of Abraham, the God of Isaac, and the God of Jacob. (Exodus 3:6)

Pause to express your thoughts of praise and worship.

Personal Examination

O LORD, don't rebuke me in your anger! Don't discipline me in your rage! Your arrows have struck deep, and your blows are crushing me. Because of your anger, my whole body is sick; my health is broken because of my sins. My guilt overwhelms me—it is a burden too heavy to bear. (Psalm 38:1–4)

Ask the Spirit to search your heart and reveal any areas of unconfessed sin. Acknowledge these to the Lord and thank him for his forgiveness.

Commitment

"You must love the Lord your God with all your heart, all your soul, and all your mind." This is the first and greatest commandment. A second is equally important: "Love your neighbor as yourself." All the other commandments and all the demands of the prophets are based on these two commandments. (Matthew 22:37–40)

Let us stop just saying we love each other; let us really show it by our actions. It is by our actions that we know we are living in the truth, so we will be confident when we stand before the Lord, even if our hearts condemn us. For God is greater than our hearts, and he knows everything. Dear friends, if our conscience is clear, we can come to God with bold confidence. And we will receive whatever we request because we obey him and do the things that please him. (1 John 3:18–22)

Pause to add your own prayers for commitment and renewal.

Personal Concerns

In my deep distress, may I seek the LORD and cry out humbly to God. When I pray, please listen to me and hear my request for help. May I remember that you alone are God! (2 Chronicles 33:12–13)

Growth in Character
Pause to look to the Lord for the power to stand firm in the spiritual warfare against the world, the flesh, and spiritual forces of wickedness. Ask that you would grow in character

and pursue the disciplines of the faith in a spirit of radical dependence upon him.

Concerns for Others

We should share each other's troubles and problems, and in this way obey the law of Christ. (Galatians 6:2)

World Affairs

Lift up the needs of the poor and the hungry, the oppressed and the persecuted. Pray for those in positions of authority and ask for the blessings of peace rather than conflict.

Prayer of Thanksgiving

We have all benefited from the rich blessings he brought to us—one gracious blessing after another. For the law was given through Moses; God's unfailing love and faithfulness came through Jesus Christ. (John 1:16–17)

Jesus is the Lamb of God, who takes away the sin of the world. (John 1:29)

Pause to offer your own expressions of thanksgiving.

Concluding Prayer

Why am I discouraged? Why so sad? I will put my hope in God! I will praise him again—my Savior and my God! Now I am deeply discouraged, but I will remember your kindness. (Psalm 42:5–6, 11)

Day 22

Praise and Worship

I will rejoice in the LORD. I will be glad because he rescues me. (Psalm 35:9)

O God, you are my God; I earnestly search for you. My soul thirsts for you; my whole body longs for you in this parched and weary land where there is no water. (Psalm 63:1)

Pause to express your thoughts of praise and worship.

Personal Examination

Forgive me, though I've neglected the Rock who fathered me and me birth. (Deuteronomy 32:18)

Ask the Spirit to search your heart and reveal any areas of unconfessed sin. Acknowledge these to the Lord and thank him for his forgiveness.

Commitment

God blesses those who realize their need for him, for the Kingdom of Heaven is given to them. God blesses those who mourn, for they will be comforted. God blesses those who are gentle and lowly, for the whole earth will belong to them. (Matthew 5:3–5)

God blesses those who are hungry and thirsty for justice, for they will receive it in full. (Matthew 5:6)

God blesses those who are merciful, for they will be shown mercy. (Matthew 5:7)

May these beatitudes become a reality in my life.
Pause to add your own prayers for commitment and renewal.

Personal Concerns

May I be strong and courageous! May I not be afraid or discouraged. For the LORD my God is with me wherever I go. (Joshua 1:9)

Knowing, Loving, and Trusting God
Pause to ask God for the grace to know and please him. Ask him to enlarge your capacity to love him more and abide wholly in him.

Concerns for Others

But you are not like that, for you are a chosen people. You are a kingdom of priests, God's holy nation, his very own possession. This is so you can show others the goodness of God, for he called you out of the darkness into his wonderful light. Once you were not a people; now you are the people of God. Once you received none of God's mercy; now you have received his mercy. (1 Peter 2:9–10)

Churches and Ministries
Ask God to work on behalf of the people and concerns at your local church. Pray for his blessing and power in the ministries

that are engaged in Christian witness, discipleship, education, and those serving people in need.

Prayer of Thanksgiving

I will thank the LORD because he is just; I will sing praise to the name of the LORD Most High. (Psalm 7:17)

The LORD is my light and my salvation—so why should I be afraid? The LORD protects me from danger—so why should I tremble? (Psalm 27:1)

Pause to offer your own expressions of thanksgiving.

Concluding Prayer

The word of God is full of living power. It is sharper than the sharpest knife, cutting deep into our innermost thoughts and desires. It exposes us for what we really are. Nothing in all creation can hide from him. Everything is naked and exposed before his eyes. This is the God to whom we must explain all that we have done. (Hebrews 4:12–13)

May I continue to build my life on the foundation of my holy faith. May I continue to pray as I am directed by the Holy Spirit. May I live in such a way that God's love can bless me as I wait for the eternal life that our Lord Jesus Christ in his mercy is going to give me. (Jude 20–21)

Day 23

Praise and Worship

Do people know where to find wisdom? Where can they find understanding? It is hidden from the eyes of all humanity. Even the sharp-eyed birds in the sky cannot discover it. But Destruction and Death say, "We have heard a rumor of where wisdom can be found." God surely knows where it can be found, for he looks throughout the whole earth, under all the heavens. (Job 28:20–24)

No wonder people everywhere fear you. People who are truly wise show you reverence. (Job 37:24)

Pause to express your thoughts of praise and worship.

Personal Examination

Fire tests the purity of silver and gold, but the LORD tests the heart. (Proverbs 17:3)

Ask the Spirit to search your heart and reveal any areas of unconfessed sin. Acknowledge these to the Lord and thank him for his forgiveness.

Commitment

You must be careful to obey all of my laws and regulations, for I am the LORD. (Leviticus 19:37)

When I make decisions, I will never favor those who are rich; but be fair to lowly and great alike. I will not be afraid of how they will react, for I am judging in the place of God. (Deuteronomy 1:17)

Pause to add your own prayers for commitment and renewal.

Personal Concerns

God blesses those whose hearts are pure, for they will see God. God blesses those who work for peace, for they will be called the children of God. (Matthew 5:8–9)

God blesses those who are persecuted because they live for God, for the Kingdom of Heaven is theirs. God blesses you when you are mocked and persecuted and lied about because you are my followers. Be happy about it! Be very glad! For a great reward awaits you in heaven. And remember, the ancient prophets were persecuted, too. (Matthew 5:10–12)

May these beatitudes become a reality in my life.

Greater Wisdom

Pause to ask God for the grace to develop an eternal perspective on your life and concerns, and that he would renew your mind with his truth. Ask for the power to order your steps with wisdom and skill in each area of life so that you will seek to please him rather than impress others.

Concerns for Others

The Lord told the apostles, "When the Holy Spirit has come upon you, you will receive power and will tell people about me everywhere—in Jerusalem, through-out Judea, in Samaria, and to the ends of the earth." (Acts 1:8)

Loved Ones

Lift up the members of your immediate family and your extended family. Pray for the spiritual, emotional, and physical concerns of your loved ones.

Prayer of Thanksgiving

Praise the LORD; praise God our savior! For each day he carries us in his arms. Our God is a God who saves! The Sovereign LORD rescues us from death. (Psalm 68:19–20)

It is good to give thanks to the LORD, to sing praises to the Most High. It is good to proclaim your unfailing love in the morning, your faithfulness in the evening. (Psalm 92:1–2)

Pause to offer your own expressions of thanksgiving.

Concluding Prayer

You give power to those who are tired and worn out; you offer strength to the weak. Even youths will be-come exhausted, and young men will give up. But those who wait on the LORD will find new strength. They will fly high on wings like eagles. They will run and not grow weary. They will walk and not faint. (Isaiah 40:29–31)

Day 24

Praise and Worship

God made the earth by his power, and he preserves it by his wisdom. He has stretched out the heavens by his understanding. (Jeremiah 10:12; 51:15)

It is the LORD who provides the sun to light the day and the moon and stars to light the night. It is he who stirs the sea into roaring waves. His name is the LORD Almighty. (Jeremiah 31:35)

Pause to express your thoughts of praise and worship.

Personal Examination

We have sinned. We have done wrong! We have acted wickedly! (Psalm 106:6)

Ask the Spirit to search your heart and reveal any areas of unconfessed sin. Acknowledge these to the Lord and thank him for his forgiveness.

Commitment

May I love my enemies and pray for those who persecute me! (Matthew 5:44)

May I do for others what I would like them to do for me. This is a summary of all that is taught in the law and the prophets. (Matthew 7:12)

Pause to add your own prayers for commitment and renewal.

Personal Concerns

I look to you for help, O Sovereign LORD. You are my refuge. (Psalm 141:8)

Spiritual Insight

Pause to ask that the Holy Spirit would give you understanding and insight into the word of truth, so that you will have a growing grasp of your identity in Christ—where you came from, who you are, and where you are going. Ask for a clearer understanding of God's purpose for your life.

Concerns for Others

Those who oppress the poor insult their Maker, but those who help the poor honor him. (Proverbs 14:31)

Other Believers

Intercede in the lives of your personal friends, and ask that the Lord will bless their families, their careers, and their ministries. Pray that he will comfort and strengthen those who are oppressed and in need.

Prayer of Thanksgiving

The LORD helps the fallen and lifts up those bent beneath their loads. All eyes look to you for help; you give them their food as they need it. When you open your hand, you satisfy the hunger and thirst of every living thing. (Psalm 145:14–16)

Pause to offer your own expressions of thanksgiving.

Concluding Prayer

Praise the LORD! Praise the LORD from the heavens! Praise him from the skies! Praise him, all his angels! Praise him, all the armies of heaven! Praise him, sun and moon! Praise him, all you twinkling stars! Praise him, skies above! Praise him, vapors high above the clouds! Let every created thing give praise to the LORD, for he issued his command, and they came into being. He established them forever and forever. His orders will never be revoked. (Psalm 148:1–6)

Day 25

Praise and Worship

In the beginning the Word already existed. He was with God, and he was God. He was in the beginning with God. (John 1:1–2)

There is only one God, the Father, who created everything, and I exist for him. And there is only one Lord, Jesus Christ, through whom God made everything and through whom I have been given life. (1 Corinthians 8:6)

Pause to express your thoughts of praise and worship.

Personal Examination

What is more pleasing to the LORD: your burnt offerings and sacrifices or your obedience to his voice? Obedience is far better than sacrifice. Listening to him is much better than offering the fat of rams. Rebellion is as bad as the sin of witchcraft, and stubbornness is as bad as worshiping idols. So because you have rejected the word of the LORD, he has rejected you from being king. (1 Samuel 15:22–23)

Ask the Spirit to search your heart and reveal any areas of unconfessed sin. Acknowledge these to the Lord and thank him for his forgiveness.

Commitment

Dear friends, don't be afraid of those who want to kill you. They can only kill the body; they cannot do any more to you. But I'll tell you whom to fear. Fear God, who has the power to kill people and then throw them into hell. (Luke 12:4–5)

You must fear the LORD your God and serve him. When you take an oath, you must use only his name. (Deuteronomy 6:13)

May I be very careful to obey all the commands and the law that Moses gave to you. May I love the LORD my God, walk in all his ways, obey his commands, be faithful to him, and serve him with all my heart and all my soul. (Joshua 22:5)

Pause to add your own prayers for commitment and renewal.

Personal Concerns

May I not join a crowd that intends to do evil. When I am on the witness stand, may I not be swayed in my testimony by the opinion of the majority. (Exodus 23:2)

May I take no bribes, for a bribe makes you ignore something that you clearly see. A bribe always hurts the cause of the person who is in the right. (Exodus 23:8)

Love and Compassion

Pause to ask for the grace of greater love and compassion for others. Pray that you will become a more Christlike person who considers the needs of others above your own, knowing that God is your provider and sustainer.

Concerns for Others

God overlooked people's former ignorance, but now he commands everyone everywhere to turn away from idols and turn to him. For he has set a day for judging the world with justice by the man he has appointed, and he proved to everyone who this is by raising him from the dead. (Acts 17:30–31)

Christian Witness

Pray on behalf of the people you personally know who have not yet entered into the joy of a personal relationship with Jesus. Intercede for your unsaved relatives, neighbors, co-workers, and friends.

Prayer of Thanksgiving

When you created people, you made them in your likeness. You created them male and female, and you blessed them and called them "human." (Genesis 5:1–2)

God, the LORD, created the heavens and stretched them out. He created the earth and everything in it. He gives breath and life to everyone in all the world. (Isaiah 42:5)

Pause to offer your own expressions of thanksgiving.

Concluding Prayer

The LORD keeps you from all evil and preserves your life. The LORD keeps watch over you as you come and go, both now and forever. (Psalm 121:7–8)

Day 26

Praise and Worship

May I fear the LORD my God and worship him and cling to him. My oaths must be in his name alone. He is my God, the one who is worthy of my praise, the one who has done mighty miracles that I myself have seen. (Deuteronomy 10:20–21)

You are our God, the great and mighty and awesome God, who keeps his covenant of unfailing love. (Nehemiah 9:32)

Pause to express your thoughts of praise and worship.

Personal Examination

O my God, I am utterly ashamed; I blush to lift up my face to you. For my sins are piled higher than my head, and my guilt has reached to the heavens. (Ezra 9:6)

Ask the Spirit to search your heart and reveal any areas of unconfessed sin. Acknowledge these to the Lord and thank him for his forgiveness.

Commitment

May I fear God and obey his commands, for this is the duty of every person. (Ecclesiastes 12:13)

Give me understanding and I will obey your law; I will put it into practice with all my heart. Make me walk along the path of your commands, for that is where my happiness is found. Give me an eagerness for your decrees; do not inflict me with love for money! Turn my eyes from worthless things, and give me life through your word. (Psalm 119:34–37)

Pause to add your own prayers for commitment and renewal.

Personal Concerns

Like Ezra, I want to study and obey the law of the LORD and teach those laws and regulations to others. (Ezra 7:10)

Faithfulness as a Steward

Pause to ask that God would empower you to become a more faithful and effective steward with all that he has entrusted to your care. Since he has given you a stewardship of talents, treasure, truth, time, and love and compassion, ask that you would use these gifts with fidelity in his service.

Concerns for Others

The kind of fasting I want calls you to free those who are wrongly imprisoned and to stop oppressing those who work for you. Treat them fairly and give them what they earn. I want you to share your food with the hungry and to welcome poor wanderers into your homes. Give clothes to those who need them, and do not hide from relatives who need your help. If you do these things, your salvation will come like the dawn. Yes, your healing will come quickly. Your godliness will lead you forward, and the glory of the LORD will protect you from behind. (Isaiah 58:6–8)

Government

Lift up those in local, state, and national government, and pray that those in positions of authority would look to God for wisdom in their decisions and practice.

Prayer of Thanksgiving

The heavens tell of the glory of God. The skies display his marvelous craftsmanship. Day after day they continue to speak; night after night they make him known. (Psalm 19:1–2)

I will praise you, LORD, for you have rescued me. You refused to let my enemies triumph over me. O LORD my God, I cried out to you for help, and you restored my health. (Psalm 30:1–2)

Pause to offer your own expressions of thanksgiving.

Concluding Prayer

Who else among the gods is like you, O LORD? Who is glorious in holiness like you—so awesome in splendor, performing such wonders? (Exodus 15:11)

No one is holy like you, LORD! There is no one besides you; there is no Rock like our God. (1 Samuel 2:2)

Day 27

Praise and Worship

Great is the LORD! He is most worthy of praise! He is to be revered above all the gods. The gods of other nations are merely idols, but the LORD made the heavens! Honor and majesty surround him; strength and beauty are in his sanctuary. O nations of the world, recognize the LORD; recognize that the LORD is glorious and strong. Give to the LORD the glory he deserves! Bring your offering and come to worship him. (Psalm 96:4–8)

Praise the LORD! Happy are those who fear the LORD. Yes, happy are those who delight in doing what he commands. (Psalm 112:1)

Pause to express your thoughts of praise and worship.

Personal Examination

I know that you are a gracious and compassionate God, slow to get angry and filled with unfailing love. I know how easily you cancel your plans for destruction. (Jonah 4:2)

Ask the Spirit to search your heart and reveal any areas of unconfessed sin. Acknowledge these to the Lord and thank him for his forgiveness.

Commitment

The most important commandment is this: "Hear, O Israel! The Lord our God is the one and only Lord." And you must love the Lord your God with all your heart, all your soul, all your mind, and all your strength. The second is equally important: "Love your neighbor as yourself." No other commandment is greater than these. And I know it is important to love him with all my heart and all my understanding and all my strength, and to love my neighbors as myself. This is more important than to offer all of the burnt offerings and sacrifices required in the law. (Mark 12:29–31, 33)

Pause to add your own prayers for commitment and renewal.

Personal Concerns

From the depths of despair, O LORD, I call for your help. Hear my cry, O LORD. Pay attention to my prayer. (Psalm 130:1–2)

Family and Ministry

Pause to lift up your family, your career, and your ministry before the Lord. Ask that you would have the privilege of sharing Christ with others and helping people grow in their knowledge of him.

Concerns for Others

God saved you by his special favor when you believed. And you can't take credit for this; it is a gift from God. Salvation is not a reward for the good things we have done, so none of us can boast about it. For we are God's masterpiece. He has created us anew in Christ Jesus, so that we can do the good things he planned for us long ago. (Ephesians 2:8–10)

Missions

Intercede for national and world missions, and pray that those who have dedicated their lives to the fulfillment of the Great Commission will be strengthened, encouraged, and empowered.

Prayer of Thanksgiving

How we thank God, who gives us victory over sin and death through Jesus Christ our Lord! So, my dear brothers and sisters, be strong and steady, always enthusiastic about the Lord's work, for you know that nothing you do for the Lord is ever useless. (1 Corinthians 15:57–58)

Pause to offer your own expressions of thanksgiving.

Concluding Prayer

You are the Alpha and the Omega—the Beginning and the End. To all who are thirsty you will give the springs of the water of life without charge! All who are victorious will inherit all these blessings, and you will be their God, and they will be your children. (Revelation 21:6–7)

You are coming soon, and your reward is with you, to repay all according to their deeds. You are the Alpha and the Omega, the First and the Last, the Beginning and the End. He who is the faithful witness to all these things says, "Yes, I am coming soon!" Amen! Come, Lord Jesus. (Revelation 22:12–13, 20)

Day 28

Praise and Worship

Your throne, O God, endures forever and ever. Your royal power is expressed in justice. You love what is right and hate what is wrong. Therefore God, your God, has anointed you, pouring out the oil of joy on you more than on anyone else. (Psalm 45:6–7)

Let each generation tell its children of your mighty acts. I will meditate on your majestic, glorious splendor and your wonderful miracles. Your awe-inspiring deeds will be on every tongue; I will proclaim your greatness. (Psalm 145:4–6)

Pause to express your thoughts of praise and worship.

Personal Examination

All who fear the LORD will hate evil. That is why I hate pride, arrogance, corruption, and perverted speech. (Proverbs 8:13)

Ask the Spirit to search your heart and reveal any areas of unconfessed sin. Acknowledge these to the Lord and thank him for his forgiveness.

Commitment

May I not worship any other gods besides you. (Exodus 20:3; Deuteronomy 5:7)

May I not make for myself an idol of any kind. (Exodus 20:4; Deuteronomy 5:8)

May I not misuse the name of the LORD my God. The LORD will not let you go unpunished if you misuse his name. (Exodus 20:7; Deuteronomy 5:11)

Pause to add your own prayers for commitment and renewal.

Personal Concerns

May I be an honest person who fears God and hates bribes. (Exodus 18:21)

Growth in Character

Pause to look to the Lord for the power to stand firm in the spiritual warfare against the world, the flesh, and spiritual forces of wickedness. Ask that you would grow in character and pursue the disciplines of the faith in a spirit of radical dependence upon him.

Concerns for Others

Do not rob the poor because they are poor or exploit the needy in court. For the LORD is their defender. He will injure anyone who injures them. (Proverbs 22:22–23)

World Affairs

Lift up the needs of the poor and the hungry, the oppressed and the persecuted. Pray for those in positions of authority and ask for the blessings of peace rather than conflict.

Prayer of Thanksgiving

I pray that I will begin to understand the incredible greatness of your power for me, because I believe you. This is the same mighty power that raised Christ from the dead and seated him in the place of honor at God's right hand in the heavenly realms. Now he is far above any ruler or authority or power or leader or anything else in this world or in the world to come. (Ephesians 1:19–21)

God is so rich in mercy, and he loves us so very much, that even while we were dead because of our sins, he gave us life when he raised Christ from the dead. (It is only by God's special favor that you have been saved!) (Ephesians 2:4–5)

Pause to offer your own expressions of thanksgiving.

Concluding Prayer

The LORD is for me, so I will not be afraid. What can mere mortals do to me? It is better to trust the LORD than to put confidence in people. It is better to trust the LORD than to put confidence in princes. (Psalm 118:6, 8–9)

I look up to the mountains—does my help come from there? My help comes from the LORD, who made the heavens and the earth! He will not let you stumble and fall; the one who watches over you will not sleep. The LORD himself watches over you! The LORD stands beside you as your protective shade. The sun will not hurt you by day, nor the moon at night. (Psalm 121:1–3, 5–6)

Day 29

Praise and Worship

When I learn your righteous laws, I will thank you by living as I should! (Psalm 119:7)

I know the greatness of the LORD—that our LORD is greater than any other god. The LORD does whatever pleases him throughout all heaven and earth, and on the seas and in their depths. (Psalm 135:5–6)

Pause to express your thoughts of praise and worship.

Personal Examination

What can I say to you? How can I plead? How can I prove my innocence? (Genesis 44:16)

Ask the Spirit to search your heart and reveal any areas of unconfessed sin. Acknowledge these to the Lord and thank him for his forgiveness.

Commitment

Since I died with Christ, I know I will also share his new life. I am sure of this because Christ rose from the dead, and he will never die again. Death no longer has any power over him. He died once to defeat sin, and now he lives for the glory of God. So I should consider myself dead to sin and able to live for the glory of God through Christ Jesus. (Romans 6:8–11)

After starting my Christian life in the Spirit, may I not try to become perfect by my own human effort? (Galatians 3:3)

Pause to add your own prayers for commitment and renewal.

Personal Concerns

Oh, that you would bless me and extend my lands! Please be with me in all I do and keep me from trouble and pain. (1 Chronicles 4:10)

Knowing, Loving, and Trusting God

Pause to ask God for the grace to know and please him. Ask him to enlarge your capacity to love him more and abide wholly in him.

Concerns for Others

Anyone who loves other Christians is living in the light and does not cause anyone to stumble. Anyone who hates a Christian brother or sister is living and walking in darkness. Such a person is lost, having been blinded by the darkness. (1 John 2:10–11)

Churches and Ministries

Ask God to work on behalf of the people and concerns at your local church. Pray for his blessing and power in the ministries that are engaged in Christian witness, discipleship, education, and those serving people in need.

Prayer of Thanksgiving

God showed his love and kindness to us through Christ Jesus. And now he has made all of this plain to us by the coming of Christ Jesus, our Savior, who broke the power of death and showed us the way to everlasting life through the Good News. (2 Timothy 1:9b–10)

Oh, how kind and gracious the Lord was! He filled me completely with faith and the love of Christ Jesus. (1 Timothy 1:14)

Pause to offer your own expressions of thanksgiving.

Concluding Prayer

God made all the stars—the Bear, Orion, the Pleiades, and the constellations of the southern sky. His great works are too marvelous to understand. He performs miracles without number. (Job 9:9–10)

When I look at the night sky and see the work of your fingers—the moon and the stars you have set in place—what are mortals that you should think of us, mere humans that you should care for us? For you made us only a little lower than God, and you crowned us with glory and honor. You put us in charge of everything you made, giving us authority over all things. (Psalm 8:3–6)

Day 30

Praise and Worship

The LORD my God is a devouring fire, a jealous God. (Deuteronomy 4:24)

The LORD is sitting on his throne with all the armies of heaven around him, on his right and on his left. (1 Kings 22:19)

Not even the highest heavens can contain the LORD. (2 Chronicles 2:6; 6:18)

Pause to express your thoughts of praise and worship.

Personal Examination

Have mercy on me, O God, because of your unfailing love. Because of your great compassion, blot out the stain of my sins. Wash me clean from my guilt. Purify me from my sin. For I recognize my shameful deeds—they haunt me day and night. Against you, and you alone, have I sinned; I have done what is evil in your sight. You will be proved right in what you say, and your judgment against me is just. (Psalm 51:1–4)

Ask the Spirit to search your heart and reveal any areas of unconfessed sin. Acknowledge these to the Lord and thank him for his forgiveness.

Commitment

May I not lose sight of good planning and insight. May I hang on to them, for they fill me with life and bring me honor and respect. (Proverbs 3:21–22)

May I study your Book continually and meditate on it day and night so I may be sure to obey all that is written in it. Only then will I succeed. (Joshua 1:8)

Pause to add your own prayers for commitment and renewal.

Personal Concerns

May I follow your laws and regulations and be careful to observe them, for this is my wisdom and intelligence in the sight of others. (Deuteronomy 4:5–6)

Greater Wisdom
Pause to ask God for the grace to develop an eternal perspective on your life and concerns, and that he would renew your mind with his truth. Ask for the power to order your steps with wisdom and skill in each area of life so that you will seek to please him rather than impress others.

Concerns for Others

Oh, that they would always have hearts like this, that they might fear me and obey all my commands! If they did, they and their descendants would prosper forever. (Deuteronomy 5:29)

Loved Ones

Lift up the members of your immediate family and your extended family. Pray for the spiritual, emotional, and physical concerns of your loved ones.

Prayer of Thanksgiving

The LORD is close to the brokenhearted; he rescues those who are crushed in spirit. The righteous face many troubles, but the LORD rescues them from each and every one. (Psalm 34:18–19)

God is our refuge and strength, always ready to help in times of trouble. So we will not fear, even if earthquakes come and the mountains crumble into the sea. (Psalm 46:1–2)

Pause to offer your own expressions of thanksgiving.

Concluding Prayer

"I know the plans I have for you," says the LORD. "They are plans for good and not for disaster, to give you a future and a hope." (Jeremiah 29:11)

You left me with a gift—peace of mind and heart. And the peace you give isn't like the peace the world gives. So I won't be troubled or afraid. (John 14:27)

Day 31

Praise and Worship

Everyone will share the story of your wonderful goodness; they will sing with joy of your righteousness. The LORD is kind and merciful, slow to get angry, full of unfailing love. The LORD is good to everyone. He showers compassion on all his creation. (Psalm 145:7–9)

Pause to express your thoughts of praise and worship.

Personal Examination

I—yes, I alone—am the one who blots out your sins for my own sake and will never think of them again. (Isaiah 43:25)

Ask the Spirit to search your heart and reveal any areas of unconfessed sin. Acknowledge these to the Lord and thank him for his forgiveness.

Commitment

I am the salt of the earth. But what good is salt if it has lost its flavor? Can you make it useful again? It will be thrown out and trampled underfoot as worthless. I am the light of the world—like a city on a mountain, glowing in the night for all to see. I won't hide my light under a basket! Instead, I will put it on a stand and let it shine for all. In the same way, I will let my good deeds shine out for all to see, so that everyone will praise my heavenly Father. (Matthew 5:13–16)

Pause to add your own prayers for commitment and renewal.

Personal Concerns

May I never avenge myself. I will leave that to God. For it is written, "I will take vengeance; I will repay those who deserve it," says the Lord. Don't let evil get the best of you, but conquer evil by doing good. (Romans 12:19, 21)

Spiritual Insight

Pause to ask that the Holy Spirit would give you understanding and insight into the word of truth, so that you will have a growing grasp of your identity in Christ—where you came from, who you are, and where you are going. Ask for a clearer understanding of God's purpose for your life.

Concerns for Others

Is there any encouragement from belonging to Christ? Any comfort from his love? Any fellowship together in the Spirit? Are your hearts tender and sympathetic? Then make me truly happy by agreeing wholeheartedly with each other, loving one another, and working together with one heart and purpose. Don't be selfish; don't live to make a good impression on others. Be humble, thinking of others as better than yourself. Don't think only about your own affairs, but be interested in others, too, and what they are doing. (Philippians 2:1–4)

Other Believers

Intercede in the lives of your personal friends, and ask that the Lord will bless their families, their careers, and their ministries. Pray that he will comfort and strengthen those who are oppressed and in need.

Prayer of Thanksgiving

Shout for joy, O heavens! Rejoice, O earth! Burst into song, O mountains! For the LORD has comforted his people and will have compassion on them in their sorrow. (Isaiah 49:13)

I am overwhelmed with joy in the LORD my God! For he has dressed me with the clothing of salvation and draped me in a robe of righteousness. I am like a bridegroom in his wedding suit or a bride with her jewels. (Isaiah 61:10)

Pause to offer your own expressions of thanksgiving.

Concluding Prayer

God comforts us in all our troubles so that we can comfort others. When others are troubled, we will be able to give them the same comfort God has given us. (2 Corinthians 1:4)

Satisfy us in the morning with your unfailing love, so we may sing for joy to the end of our lives. (Psalm 90:14)

The Second Month

Day 1

Praise and Worship

God stretches the northern sky over empty space and hangs the earth on nothing. (Job 26:7)

It is the LORD who created the stars, the Pleiades and Orion. It is he who turns darkness into morning and day into night. It is he who draws up water from the oceans and pours it down as rain on the land. The LORD is his name! (Amos 5:8)

Pause to express your thoughts of praise and worship.

Personal Examination

Please, LORD, prove that your power is as great as you have claimed it to be. For you said, the LORD is slow to anger and rich in unfailing love, forgiving every kind of sin and rebellion. Even so he does not leave sin unpunished, but he punishes the children for the sins of their parents to the third and fourth generations. (Numbers 14:17–18)

Ask the Spirit to search your heart and reveal any areas of unconfessed sin. Acknowledge these to the Lord and thank him for his forgiveness.

Commitment

By your grace, I want to hear the words, "Well done my good and faithful servant. You have been faithful in handling this small amount, so now I will give you many more responsibilities. Let's celebrate together!" (Matthew 25:21)

May I not love human praise more than the praise of God. (John 12:43)

I am the Lord's servant; I am willing to accept whatever he wants. (Luke 1:38)

Pause to add your own prayers for commitment and renewal.

Personal Concerns

Don't you know that your body is the temple of the Holy Spirit, who lives in you and was given to you by God? You do not belong to yourself, for God bought you with a high price. So you must honor God with your body. (1 Corinthians 6:19–20)

Knowing, Loving, and Trusting God
Pause to ask God for the grace to know and please him. Ask him to enlarge your capacity to love him more and abide wholly in him.

Concerns for Others

Give fair judgment to the poor and the orphan; uphold the rights of the oppressed and the destitute. Rescue the poor and helpless; deliver them from the grasp of evil people. (Psalm 82:3–4)

Churches and Ministries

Ask God to work on behalf of the people and concerns at your local church. Pray for his blessing and power in the ministries that are engaged in Christian witness, discipleship, education, and those serving people in need.

Prayer of Thanksgiving

Understand, therefore, that the LORD your God is indeed God. He is the faithful God who keeps his covenant for a thousand generations and constantly loves those who love him and obey his commands. (Deuteronomy 7:9)

I will tell of the LORD's unfailing love. I will praise the LORD for all he has done. I will rejoice in his great goodness to Israel, which he has granted according to his mercy and love. (Isaiah 63:7)

Pause to offer your own expressions of thanksgiving.

Concluding Prayer

Tell them, "The LORD, the God of your ancestors—the God of Abraham, the God of Isaac, and the God of Jacob—has sent me to you." This will be my name forever; it has always been my name, and it will be used throughout all generations. (Exodus 3:15)

Then Moses and the people of Israel sang this song to the LORD: "I will sing to the LORD, for he has triumphed gloriously; he has thrown both horse and rider into the sea. The LORD is my strength and my song; he has become my victory. He is my God, and I will praise him; he is my father's God, and I will exalt him!" (Exodus 15:1–2)

Day 2

Praise and Worship

The LORD is the only true God, the living God. He is the everlasting King! The whole earth trembles at his anger. The nations hide before his wrath. (Jeremiah 10:10)

How great are God's signs, how powerful his wonders! His kingdom will last forever, his rule through all generations. (Daniel 4:3)

Pause to express your thoughts of praise and worship.

Personal Examination

God carefully watches the way people live; he sees everything they do. No darkness is thick enough to hide the wicked from his eyes. For it is not up to mortals to decide when to come before God in judgment. (Job 34:21–23)

Ask the Spirit to search your heart and reveal any areas of unconfessed sin. Acknowledge these to the Lord and thank him for his forgiveness.

Commitment

May I remove the places of idolatry from my life, and like Asa remain fully committed to the LORD throughout my life. (2 Chronicles 15:17)

Trust in the LORD and do good. Then you will live safely in the land and prosper. Take delight in the LORD, and he will give you your heart's desires. Commit everything you do to the LORD. Trust him, and he will help you. He will make your innocence as clear as the dawn, and the justice of your cause will shine like the noonday sun. Be still in the presence of the LORD, and wait patiently for him to act. Don't worry about evil people who prosper or fret about their wicked schemes. (Psalm 37:3–7)

He must become greater and greater, and I must become less and less. (John 3:30)

Pause to add your own prayers for commitment and renewal.

Personal Concerns

May I follow Abraham's example of willingness to offer all that I have to you, holding nothing back and trusting in your character and in your promises. (Genesis 22:2–12, 16)

Greater Wisdom

Pause to ask God for the grace to develop an eternal perspective on your life and concerns, and that he would renew your mind with his truth. Ask for the power to order your steps with wisdom and skill in each area of life so that you will seek to please him rather than impress others.

Concerns for Others

O people, the LORD has already told you what is good, and this is what he requires: to do what is right, to love mercy, and to walk humbly with your God. (Micah 6:8)

Loved Ones

Lift up the members of your immediate family and your extended family. Pray for the spiritual, emotional, and physical concerns of your loved ones.

Prayer of Thanksgiving

No longer will anything be cursed. For the throne of God and of the Lamb will be there, and his servants will worship him. And they will see his face, and his name will be written on their foreheads. And there will be no night there—no need for lamps or sun—for the Lord God will shine on them. And they will reign forever and ever. (Revelation 22:3–5)

Pause to offer your own expressions of thanksgiving.

Concluding Prayer

Praise the name of God forever and ever, for he alone has all wisdom and power. He determines the course of world events; he removes kings and sets others on the throne. He gives wisdom to the wise and knowledge to the scholars. He reveals deep and mysterious things and knows what lies hidden in darkness, though he himself is surrounded by light. God is wise and powerful! (Daniel 2:20–22)

Day 3

Praise and Worship

Praise the LORD! Give thanks to the LORD, for he is good! His faithful love endures forever. Who can list the glorious miracles of the LORD? Who can ever praise him half enough? (Psalm 106:1–2)

Pause to express your thoughts of praise and worship.

Personal Examination

I have heard all about you, LORD, and I am filled with awe by the amazing things you have done. In this time of my deep need, begin again to help me, as you did in years gone by. Show me your power to save me. And in your anger, remember your mercy. (Habakkuk 3:2)

Ask the Spirit to search your heart and reveal any areas of unconfessed sin. Acknowledge these to the Lord and thank him for his forgiveness.

Commitment

Like Josiah, may I do what is pleasing to the LORD, following the example of his ancestor, King David, not turning aside from doing what was right. (2 Chronicles 34:1–2)

Like Josiah, give me a tender and responsive heart, so that I will humble myself before you when I hear your word. (2 Chronicles 34:27)

May I walk in the steps of Jesus, who often withdrew to lonely places and prayed. (Mark 1:35; Luke 5:16)

Pause to add your own prayers for commitment and renewal.

Personal Concerns

Keep on asking, and you will be given what you ask for. Keep on looking, and you will find. Keep on knocking, and the door will be opened. For everyone who asks, receives. Everyone who seeks, finds. And the door is opened to everyone who knocks. (Matthew 7:7–8; Luke 11:9–10)

Spiritual Insight
Pause to ask that the Holy Spirit would give you understanding and insight into the word of truth, so that you will have a growing grasp of your identity in Christ—where you came from, who you are, and where you are going. Ask for a clearer understanding of God's purpose for your life.

Concerns for Others

Learn to do good. Seek justice. Help the oppressed. Defend the orphan. Fight for the rights of widows. (Isaiah 1:17)

Other Believers
Intercede in the lives of your personal friends, and ask that the Lord will bless their families, their careers, and their

ministries. Pray that he will comfort and strengthen those who are oppressed and in need.

Prayer of Thanksgiving

Has any nation ever heard the voice of God speaking from fire—as you did—and survived? Has any other god taken one nation for himself by rescuing it from another by means of trials, miraculous signs, wonders, war, awesome power, and terrifying acts? Yet that is what the LORD your God did for you in Egypt, right before your very eyes. He showed you these things so you would realize that the LORD is God and that there is no other god. (Deuteronomy 4:33–38)

Pause to offer your own expressions of thanksgiving.

Concluding Prayer

Whom have I in heaven but you? I desire you more than anything on earth. My health may fail, and my spirit may grow weak, but God remains the strength of my heart; he is mine forever. But those who desert him will perish, for you destroy those who abandon you. But as for me, how good it is to be near God! I have made the Sovereign LORD my shelter, and I will tell everyone about the wonderful things you do. (Psalm 73:25–28)

Day 4

Praise and Worship

What a wonderful God we have! How great are his riches and wisdom and knowledge! How impossible it is for us to understand his decisions and his methods! For who can know what the Lord is thinking? Who knows enough to be his counselor? And who could ever give him so much that he would have to pay it back? For everything comes from him; everything exists by his power and is intended for his glory. To him be glory evermore. Amen. (Romans 11:33–36)

Pause to express your thoughts of praise and worship.

Personal Examination

Forgive me for shedding blood, O God who saves; then I will joyfully sing of your forgiveness. Unseal my lips, O Lord, that I may praise you. You would not be pleased with sacrifices, or I would bring them. If I brought you a burnt offering, you would not accept it. The sacrifice you want is a broken spirit. A broken and repentant heart, O God, you will not despise. (Psalm 51:14–17)

Ask the Spirit to search your heart and reveal any areas of unconfessed sin. Acknowledge these to the Lord and thank him for his forgiveness.

Commitment

Now, Israel, what does the LORD your God require of you? He requires you to fear him, to live according to his will, to love and worship him with all your heart and soul. (Deuteronomy 10:12)

I don't mean to say that I have already achieved things or that I have already reached perfection! But I keep working toward that day when I will finally be all that Christ Jesus saved me for and wants me to be. No, I am still not all I should be, but I am focusing all my energies on this one thing: forgetting the past and looking forward to what lies ahead, I strain to reach the end of the race and receive the prize for which God, through Christ Jesus, is calling us up to heaven. (Philippians 3:12–14)

Pause to add your own prayers for commitment and renewal.

Personal Concerns

You must never twist justice or show partiality. Never accept a bribe, for bribes blind the eyes of the wise and corrupt the decisions of the godly. (Deuteronomy 16:19)

Love and Compassion

Pause to ask for the grace of greater love and compassion for others. Pray that you will become a more Christlike person who considers the needs of others above your own, knowing that God is your provider and sustainer.

Concerns for Others

Our lives are a fragrance presented by Christ to God. But this fragrance is perceived differently by those being saved and by those perishing. To those who are perishing we are a fearful smell of death and doom. But to those who are being saved we are a life-giving perfume. And who is adequate for such a task as this? (2 Corinthians 2:15–16)

Christian Witness

Pray on behalf of the people you personally know who have not yet entered into the joy of a personal relationship with Jesus. Intercede for your unsaved relatives, neighbors, co-workers, and friends.

Prayer of Thanksgiving

I have loved you, my people, with an everlasting love. With unfailing love I have drawn you to myself. (Jeremiah 31:3)

I led Israel along with my ropes of kindness and love. I lifted the yoke from his neck, and I myself stooped to feed him. (Hosea 11:4)

Pause to offer your own expressions of thanksgiving.

Concluding Prayer

Sing a new song to the LORD! Let the whole earth sing to the LORD! Sing to the LORD; bless his name. Each day proclaim the good news that he saves. Publish his glorious deeds among the nations. Tell everyone about the amazing things he does. (Psalm 96:1–3)

Day 5

Praise and Worship

The LORD your God is the God of gods and LORD of lords. He is the great God, mighty and awesome, who shows no partiality and takes no bribes. He gives justice to orphans and widows. He shows love to the foreigners living among you and gives them food and clothing. (Deuteronomy 10:17–18)

Pause to express your thoughts of praise and worship.

Personal Examination

O LORD, do not rebuke me in your anger or discipline me in your rage. Have compassion on me, LORD, for I am weak. Heal me, LORD, for my body is in agony. I am sick at heart. How long, O LORD, until you restore me? (Psalm 6:1–3)

Ask the Spirit to search your heart and reveal any areas of unconfessed sin. Acknowledge these to the Lord and thank him for his forgiveness.

Commitment

Run away from sexual sin! No other sin so clearly affects the body as this one does. For sexual immorality is a sin against your own body. (1 Corinthians 6:18)

This happened as a warning to us, so that we would not crave evil things as they did or worship idols as some of them did. For the Scriptures say, "The people celebrated with feasting and drinking, and they indulged themselves in pagan revelry. And we must not engage in sexual immorality as some of them did, causing 23,000 of them to die in one day." (1 Corinthians 10:6–8)

Pause to add your own prayers for commitment and renewal.

Personal Concerns

Always judge your neighbors fairly, neither favoring the poor nor showing deference to the rich. (Leviticus 19:15)

Faithfulness as a Steward

Pause to ask that God would empower you to become a more faithful and effective steward with all that he has entrusted to your care. Since he has given you a stewardship of talents, treasure, truth, time, and love and compassion, ask that you would use these gifts with fidelity in his service.

Concerns for Others

Oh, the joys of those who are kind to the poor. The LORD rescues them in times of trouble. The LORD protects them and keeps them alive. He gives them prosperity and rescues them from their enemies. The LORD nurses them when they are sick and eases their pain and discomfort. (Psalm 41:1–3)

Government

Lift up those in local, state, and national government, and pray that those in positions of authority would look to God for wisdom in their decisions and practice.

Prayer of Thanksgiving

I recall all you have done, O LORD; I remember your wonderful deeds of long ago. They are constantly in my thoughts. I cannot stop thinking about them. O God, your ways are holy. Is there any god as mighty as you? You are the God of miracles and wonders! You demonstrate your awesome power among the nations. You have redeemed your people by your strength, the descendants of Jacob and of Joseph by your might. (Psalm 77:11–15)

Pause to offer your own expressions of thanksgiving.

Concluding Prayer

As for me, I know that my Redeemer lives, and that he will stand upon the earth at last. And after my body has decayed, yet in my body I will see God! I will see him for myself. Yes, I will see him with my own eyes. I am overwhelmed at the thought! (Job 19:25–27)

Look, God is exalted beyond what we can understand. His years are without number. (Job 36:26)

Day 6

Praise and Worship

After this, I heard the sound of a vast crowd in heaven shouting, "Hallelujah! Salvation is from our God. Glory and power belong to him alone. His judgments are just and true. He has punished the great prostitute who corrupted the earth with her immorality, and he has avenged the murder of his servants." (Revelation 19:1–2)

Afterward the LORD spoke to Abram in a vision and said to him, "Do not be afraid, Abram, for I will protect you, and your reward will be great." (Genesis 15:1)

As for God, his way is perfect. All the LORD's promises prove true. He is a shield for all who look to him for protection. For who is God except the LORD? Who but our God is a solid rock? (Psalm 18:30–31)

Pause to express your thoughts of praise and worship.

Personal Examination

As you endure divine discipline, remember that God is treating you as his own child. Whoever heard of a child who was never disciplined? If God doesn't discipline you as he does all of his children, it means that you are illegitimate and are not really his child after all. Since we respect our earthly fathers who disciplined us, should we not all the more cheerfully submit to the discipline of our heavenly Father and live forever? (Hebrews 12:7–9)

Ask the Spirit to search your heart and reveal any areas of unconfessed sin. Acknowledge these to the Lord and thank him for his forgiveness.

Commitment

"Don't be afraid," Samuel reassured them. "You have certainly done wrong, but make sure now that you worship the LORD with all your heart and that you don't turn your back on him in any way. Don't go back to worshiping worthless idols that cannot help or rescue you—they really are useless!" (1 Samuel 12:20–21)

When you follow the desires of your flesh, your lives will produce these evil results: sexual immorality, impure thoughts, eagerness for lustful pleasure, idolatry, participation in demonic activities, hostility, quarreling, jealousy, outbursts of anger, selfish ambition, divisions, the feeling that everyone is wrong except those in your own little group, envy, drunkenness, wild parties, and other kinds of sin. Let me tell you again, as I have before, that anyone living that sort of life will not inherit the Kingdom of God. But when the Holy Spirit controls our lives, he will produce this kind of fruit in us: love, joy, peace, patience, kindness, goodness, faithfulness, gentleness, and self-control. Here there is no conflict with the law. (Galatians 5:19–23)

Pause to add your own prayers for commitment and renewal.

Personal Concerns

We can say with confidence and a clear conscience that we have been honest and sincere in all our dealings. We have depended on God's grace, not on our own earthly wisdom. That is how we have acted toward everyone, and especially toward you. (2 Corinthians 1:12)

Family and Ministry

Pause to lift up your family, your career, and your ministry before the Lord. Ask that you would have the privilege of sharing Christ with others and helping people grow in their knowledge of him.

Concerns for Others

The Spirit of the Sovereign LORD is upon me, because the LORD has appointed me to bring good news to the poor. He has sent me to comfort the brokenhearted and to announce that captives will be released and prisoners will be freed. He has sent me to tell those who mourn that the time of the LORD's favor has come, and with it, the day of God's anger against their enemies. To all who mourn in Israel, he will give beauty for ashes, joy instead of mourning, praise instead of despair. For the LORD has planted them like strong and graceful oaks for his own glory. (Isaiah 61:1–3)

Missions

Intercede for national and world missions, and pray that those who have dedicated their lives to the fulfillment of the Great Commission will be strengthened, encouraged, and empowered.

Prayer of Thanksgiving

With unfailing love you will lead this people whom you have ransomed. You will guide them in your strength to the place where your holiness dwells. You will bring them in and plant them on your own mountain—the place you have made as your home, O LORD, the sanctuary, O LORD, that your hands have made. (Exodus 15:13, 17)

I, the LORD, am your God, who brought you from the land of Egypt so you would no longer be slaves. I have lifted the yoke of slavery from your neck so you can walk free with your heads held high. (Leviticus 26:13)

Pause to offer your own expressions of thanksgiving.

Concluding Prayer

Don't be afraid, for I am with you. Do not be dismayed, for I am your God. I will strengthen you. I will help you. I will uphold you with my victorious right hand. See, all your angry enemies lie there, confused and ashamed. Anyone who opposes you will die. You will look for them in vain. They will all be gone! I am holding you by your right hand—I, the LORD your God. And I say to you, "Do not be afraid. I am here to help you." (Isaiah 41:10, 13)

I still dare to hope when I remember this: The unfailing love of the LORD never ends! By his mercies we have been kept from complete destruction. Great is his faithfulness; his mercies begin afresh each day. (Lamentations 3:21–23)

Day 7

Praise and Worship

I myself am he! There is no god other than me! I am the one who kills and gives life; I am the one who wounds and heals; no one delivers from my power! (Deuteronomy 32:39)

Do not forget the things I have done throughout history. For I am God—I alone! I am God, and there is no one else like me. (Isaiah 46:9)

The LORD God is the supreme God of the heavens above and the earth below. (Joshua 2:11)

Pause to express your thoughts of praise and worship.

Personal Examination

There are six things the LORD hates—no, seven things he detests: haughty eyes, a lying tongue, hands that kill the innocent, a heart that plots evil, feet that race to do wrong, a false witness who pours out lies, a person who sows discord among brothers. (Proverbs 6:16–19)

Ask the Spirit to search your heart and reveal any areas of unconfessed sin. Acknowledge these to the Lord and thank him for his forgiveness.

Commitment

May the name of the Lord Jesus be honored through my life. (Acts 19:17)

May I give my body to God, letting it be a living and holy sacrifice—the kind he will accept. When I think of what he has done for me, is this too much to ask? (Romans 12:1)

Pause to add your own prayers for commitment and renewal.

Personal Concerns

Let me hear of your unfailing love to me in the morning, for I am trusting you. Show me where to walk, for I have come to you in prayer. (Psalm 143:8)

Growth in Character

Pause to look to the Lord for the power to stand firm in the spiritual warfare against the world, the flesh, and spiritual forces of wickedness. Ask that you would grow in character and pursue the disciplines of the faith in a spirit of radical dependence upon him.

Concerns for Others

If you help the poor, you are lending to the LORD—and he will repay you! (Proverbs 19:17)

World Affairs

Lift up the needs of the poor and the hungry, the oppressed and the persecuted. Pray for those in positions of authority and ask for the blessings of peace rather than conflict.

Prayer of Thanksgiving

You know how full of love and kindness our Lord Jesus Christ was. Though he was very rich, yet for your sakes he became poor, so that by his poverty he could make you rich. (2 Corinthians 8:9)

Let us thank God for his gift that is too wonderful for words! (2 Corinthians 9:15)

Pause to offer your own expressions of thanksgiving.

Concluding Prayer

Lord, to whom would I go? You alone have the words that give eternal life. I believe them, and I know you are the Holy One of God. (John 6:68–69)

Jesus said, "I am the resurrection and the life. Those who believe in me, even though they die like everyone else, will live again. They are given eternal life for believing in me and will never perish. Do you believe this?" (John 11:25–26)

Day 8

Praise and Worship

The word of the LORD holds true, and everything he does is worthy of our trust. He loves whatever is just and good, and his unfailing love fills the earth. (Psalm 33:4–5)

Pause to express your thoughts of praise and worship.

Personal Examination

I had heard about you before, but now I have seen you with my own eyes. I take back everything I said, and I sit in dust and ashes to show my repentance. (Job 42:5–6)

Ask the Spirit to search your heart and reveal any areas of unconfessed sin. Acknowledge these to the Lord and thank him for his forgiveness.

Commitment

Let me stop putting my trust in mere humans. They are as frail as breath. How can they be of help to anyone? (Isaiah 2:22)

May I trust in you enough to demonstrate your holiness to others. (Numbers 20:12)

Pause to add your own prayers for commitment and renewal.

Personal Concerns

May I learn how to get along happily whether I have much or little. Let me know how to live on almost nothing or with everything. May I learn the secret of living in every situation, whether it is with a full stomach or empty, with plenty or little. For I can do everything with the help of Christ who gives me the strength I need. (Philippians 4:11–13)

Knowing, Loving, and Trusting God
Pause to ask God for the grace to know and please him. Ask him to enlarge your capacity to love him more and abide wholly in him.

Concerns for Others

And now God is building you, as living stones, into his spiritual temple. What's more, you are God's holy priests, who offer the spiritual sacrifices that please him because of Jesus Christ. But you are not like that, for you are a chosen people. You are a kingdom of priests, God's holy nation, his very own possession. This is so you can show others the goodness of God, for he called you out of the darkness into his wonderful light. (1 Peter 2:5, 9)

Churches and Ministries
Ask God to work on behalf of the people and concerns at your local church. Pray for his blessing and power in the ministries that are engaged in Christian witness, discipleship, education, and those serving people in need.

Prayer of Thanksgiving

Concerning the lost, Jesus said, "If you had one hundred sheep, and one of them strayed away and was lost in the wilderness, wouldn't you leave the ninety-nine others to go and search for the lost one until you found it? And then you would joyfully carry it home on your shoulders. When you arrived, you would call together your friends and neighbors to rejoice with you because your lost sheep was found. In the same way, heaven will be happier over one lost sinner who returns to God than over ninety-nine others who are righteous and haven't strayed away! In the same way, there is joy in the presence of God's angels when even one sinner repents." (Luke 15:4–7, 10)

Pause to offer your own expressions of thanksgiving.

Concluding Prayer

Be exalted, O God, above the highest heavens! May your glory shine over all the earth. I will thank you, Lord, in front of all the people. I will sing your praises among the nations. For your unfailing love is as high as the heavens. Your faithfulness reaches to the clouds. Be exalted, O God, above the highest heavens. May your glory shine over all the earth. (Psalm 57:5, 9–11)

Day 9

Praise and Worship

Your decrees are perfect; they are entirely worthy of our trust. Your justice is eternal, and your law is perfectly true. (Psalm 119:138, 142)

My heart is confident in you, O God; no wonder I can sing your praises! Wake up, my soul! Wake up, O harp and lyre! I will waken the dawn with my song. I will thank you, LORD, in front of all the people. I will sing your praises among the nations. For your unfailing love is higher than the heavens. Your faithfulness reaches to the clouds. (Psalm 108:1–4)

Pause to express your thoughts of praise and worship.

Personal Examination

Happy are those whom you discipline, LORD, and those whom you teach from your law. (Psalm 94:12)

Ask the Spirit to search your heart and reveal any areas of unconfessed sin. Acknowledge these to the Lord and thank him for his forgiveness.

Commitment

May I listen carefully to your voice and do what is right in your sight, obeying your commands and laws. (Exodus 15:26)

I can rejoice when I run into problems and trials, for I know that they are good for me—they help me learn to endure. And endurance develops strength of character in me, and character strengthens my confident expectation of salvation. And this expectation will not disappoint me. For I know how dearly God loves me, because he has given me the Holy Spirit to fill my heart with his love. (Romans 5:3–5)

Pause to add your own prayers for commitment and renewal.

Personal Concerns

If mortals die, can they live again? This thought would give me hope, and through my struggle I would eagerly wait for release. (Job 14:14)

Greater Wisdom

Pause to ask God for the grace to develop an eternal perspective on your life and concerns, and that he would renew your mind with his truth. Ask for the power to order your steps with wisdom and skill in each area of life so that you will seek to please him rather than impress others.

Concerns for Others

Victory comes from you, O LORD. May your blessings rest on your people. (Psalm 3:8)

Loved Ones

Lift up the members of your immediate family and your extended family. Pray for the spiritual, emotional, and physical concerns of your loved ones.

Prayer of Thanksgiving

Those who live in the shelter of the Most High will find rest in the shadow of the Almighty. This I declare of the LORD: He alone is my refuge, my place of safety; he is my God, and I am trusting him. (Psalm 91:1–2)

Pause to offer your own expressions of thanksgiving.

Concluding Prayer

The eyes of the LORD search the whole earth in order to strengthen those whose hearts are fully committed to him. (2 Chronicles 16:9)

I know the LORD is always with me. I will not be shaken, for he is right beside me. No wonder my heart is filled with joy, and my mouth shouts his praises! My body rests in safety. For you will not leave my soul among the dead or allow your godly one to rot in the grave. You will show me the way of life, granting me the joy of your presence and the pleasures of living with you forever. (Psalm 16:8–9, 11)

Day 10

Praise and Worship

O Lord Almighty, God of Israel, you are enthroned between the mighty cherubim! You alone are God of all the kingdoms of the earth. You alone created the heavens and the earth. (Isaiah 37:16)

The mighty God, the Lord, has spoken; he has summoned all humanity from east to west! (Psalm 50:1)

Pause to express your thoughts of praise and worship.

Personal Examination

You are the one who corrects and disciplines everyone you love. May I be diligent and turn from my indifference. (Revelation 3:19)

Ask the Spirit to search your heart and reveal any areas of unconfessed sin. Acknowledge these to the Lord and thank him for his forgiveness.

Commitment

I am truly glad! There is wonderful joy ahead, even though it is necessary for me to endure many trials for a while. These trials are only to test my faith, to show that it is strong and pure. It is being tested as fire tests and purifies gold—and my faith is far more precious to God than mere gold. So if my faith remains strong after

being tried by fiery trials, it will bring me much praise
and glory and honor on the day when Jesus Christ is
revealed to the whole world. (1 Peter 1:6–7)

Pause to add your own prayers for commitment and renewal.

Personal Concerns

May I never be ashamed to tell others about our LORD,
but may I be ready to suffer with you for the proclama-
tion of the Good News. (2 Timothy 1:8)

Spiritual Insight

*Pause to ask that the Holy Spirit would give you under-
standing and insight into the word of truth, so that you will
have a growing grasp of your identity in Christ—where you
came from, who you are, and where you are going. Ask for a
clearer understanding of God's purpose for your life.*

Concerns for Others

Do not withhold good from those who deserve it when
it's in your power to help them. If you can help your
neighbor now, don't say, "Come back tomorrow, and
then I'll help you." (Proverbs 3:27–28)

Other Believers

*Intercede in the lives of your personal friends, and ask that
the Lord will bless their families, their careers, and their
ministries. Pray that he will comfort and strengthen those
who are oppressed and in need.*

Prayer of Thanksgiving

For those who fear your name, the Sun of Righteousness will rise with healing in his wings. And we will go free, leaping with joy like calves let out to pasture. (Malachi 4:2)

Jesus fulfilled the words of the prophet Isaiah, saying: "The Spirit of the Lord is upon me, for he has appointed me to preach Good News to the poor. He has sent me to proclaim that captives will be released, that the blind will see, that the downtrodden will be freed from their oppressors, and that the time of the Lord's favor has come." (Luke 4:18–19)

Pause to offer your own expressions of thanksgiving.

Concluding Prayer

LORD, remind me how brief my time on earth will be. Remind me that my days are numbered, and that my life is fleeing away. (Psalm 39:4)

For he understands how weak we are; he knows we are only dust. Our days on earth are like grass; like wildflowers, we bloom and die. The wind blows, and we are gone—as though we had never been here. But the love of the LORD remains forever with those who fear him. His salvation extends to the children's children of those who are faithful to his covenant, of those who obey his commandments! (Psalm 103:14–18)

Day 11

Praise and Worship

How lovely is your dwelling place, O Lord Almighty. I long, yes, I faint with longing to enter the courts of the Lord. With my whole being, body and soul, I will shout joyfully to the living God. (Psalm 84:1–2)

Your righteousness, O God, reaches to the highest heavens. You have done such wonderful things. Who can compare with you, O God? (Psalm 71:19)

Pause to express your thoughts of praise and worship.

Personal Examination

People judge by outward appearance, but the Lord looks at a person's thoughts and intentions. (1 Samuel 16:7)

Ask the Spirit to search your heart and reveal any areas of unconfessed sin. Acknowledge these to the Lord and thank him for his forgiveness.

Commitment

May I be a person who really expects him to answer, for a doubtful mind is as unsettled as a wave of the sea that is driven and tossed by the wind. They can't make up their minds. They waver back and forth in everything they do. (James 1:6, 8)

May I live my life in a way that you would consider worthy. For you called me into your Kingdom to share your glory. (1 Thessalonians 2:12)

If I keep on following my flesh, I will perish. But if through the power of the Holy Spirit I turn from it and its evil deeds, I will live. All who are led by the Spirit of God are children of God. (Romans 8:13–14)

Pause to add your own prayers for commitment and renewal.

Personal Concerns

I called on your name, LORD, from deep within the well, and you heard me! You listened to my pleading; you heard my weeping! Yes, you came at my despairing cry and told me, "Do not fear." LORD, you are my lawyer! Plead my case! For you have redeemed my life. (Lamentations 3:55–58)

Love and Compassion

Pause to ask for the grace of greater love and compassion for others. Pray that you will become a more Christlike person who considers the needs of others above your own, knowing that God is your provider and sustainer.

Concerns for Others

Because of our sins, he was wounded and crushed. He was beaten that we might have peace. He was whipped, and we were healed! All of us have strayed away like sheep. We have left God's paths to follow our own.

Yet the LORD laid on him the guilt and sins of us all. (Isaiah 53:5–6)

Christian Witness

Pray on behalf of the people you personally know who have not yet entered into the joy of a personal relationship with Jesus. Intercede for your unsaved relatives, neighbors, co-workers, and friends.

Prayer of Thanksgiving

I should not be like a cowering, fearful slave. I should behave instead like God's very own child, adopted into his family—calling him "Father, dear Father." For his Holy Spirit speaks to me deep in my heart and tells me that I am God's child. (Romans 8:15–16)

Pause to offer your own expressions of thanksgiving.

Concluding Prayer

Oh, the joys of those who do not follow the advice of the wicked, or stand around with sinners, or join in with scoffers. But they delight in doing everything the LORD wants; day and night they think about his law. They are like trees planted along the riverbank, bearing fruit each season without fail. Their leaves never wither, and in all they do, they prosper. (Psalm 1:1–3)

145

Day 12

Praise and Worship

The LORD is just! He is my rock! There is nothing but goodness in him! (Psalm 92:15)

I will search for the LORD and for his strength, and keep on searching. I will think of the wonderful works he has done, the miracles and the judgments he handed down. (Psalm 105:4–5)

Pause to express your thoughts of praise and worship.

Personal Examination

Let the people turn from their wicked deeds. Let them banish from their minds the very thought of doing wrong! Let them turn to the LORD that he may have mercy on them. Yes, turn to our God, for he will abundantly pardon. (Isaiah 55:7)

Ask the Spirit to search your heart and reveal any areas of unconfessed sin. Acknowledge these to the Lord and thank him for his forgiveness.

Commitment

Put me on trial, LORD, and cross-examine me. Test my motives and affections. For I am constantly aware of your unfailing love, and I have lived according to your truth. (Psalm 26:2–3)

Plant the good seeds of righteousness, and you will harvest a crop of my love. Plow up the hard ground of your hearts, for now is the time to seek the LORD, that he may come and shower righteousness upon you. (Hosea 10:12)

Pause to add your own prayers for commitment and renewal.

Personal Concerns

You must each make up your own mind as to how much you should give. Don't give reluctantly or in response to pressure. For God loves the person who gives cheerfully. And God will generously provide all you need. Then you will always have everything you need and plenty left over to share with others. As the Scriptures say, "Godly people give generously to the poor. Their good deeds will never be forgotten." (2 Corinthians 9:7–9)

Faithfulness as a Steward

Pause to ask that God would empower you to become a more faithful and effective steward with all that he has entrusted to your care. Since he has given you a stewardship of talents, treasure, truth, time, and love and compassion, ask that you would use these gifts with fidelity in his service.

Concerns for Others

You must never think that it was your own strength and energy that made you wealthy. Always remember that it is the LORD your God who gives you power to become rich, and he does it to fulfill the covenant he made with your ancestors. (Deuteronomy 8:17–18)

Government

Lift up those in local, state, and national government, and pray that those in positions of authority would look to God for wisdom in their decisions and practice.

Prayer of Thanksgiving

I never give up. Though my body is dying, my spirit is being renewed every day. My present troubles are quite small and won't last very long. Yet they produce for me an immeasurably great glory that will last forever! I don't look at the troubles I can see right now; rather, I look forward to what I have not yet seen. The troubles I see will soon be over, but the joys to come will last forever. (2 Corinthians 4:16–18)

Pause to offer your own expressions of thanksgiving.

Concluding Prayer

And we know that God causes everything to work together for the good of those who love God and are called according to his purpose for them. (Romans 8:28)

What can we say about such wonderful things as these? If God is for us, who can ever be against us? Since God did not spare even his own Son but gave him up for us all, won't God, who gave us Christ, also give us everything else? Who dares accuse us whom God has chosen for his own? Will God? No! He is the one who has given us right standing with himself. (Romans 8:31–32)

Day 13

Praise and Worship

The LORD Almighty is exalted by his justice. The holiness of God is displayed by his righteousness. (Isaiah 5:16)

The LORD waits for you to come to him so he can show you his love and compassion. For the LORD is a faithful God. Blessed are those who wait for him to help them. (Isaiah 30:18)

Pause to express your thoughts of praise and worship.

Personal Examination

A person's wickedness will punish him. He will see what an evil, bitter thing it is to forsake the LORD, having no fear of him. (Jeremiah 2:19)

Ask the Spirit to search your heart and reveal any areas of unconfessed sin. Acknowledge these to the Lord and thank him for his forgiveness.

Commitment

Another reason for right living is that I know how late it is; time is running out. May I wake up, for the coming of our salvation is nearer now than when we first believed. The night is almost gone; the day of salvation will soon be here. May I not live in darkness. May I get rid of my evil deeds, shed them like dirty clothes. May I clothe myself with the armor of right living, as those who live in the light. (Romans 13:11–12)

I am human, but I don't wage war with human plans and methods. I use God's mighty weapons, not mere worldly weapons, to knock down the Devil's strongholds. With these weapons I break down every proud argument that keeps people from knowing God. With these weapons I conquer their rebellious ideas and teach them to obey Christ. (2 Corinthians 10:3–5)

Pause to add your own prayers for commitment and renewal.

Personal Concerns

Since God chose me to be one of his holy people whom he loves, I must clothe myself with tenderhearted mercy, kindness, humility, gentleness, and patience. I must make allowance for other's faults and forgive the person who offends me. I remember, the Lord forgave me, so I must forgive others. And the most important piece of clothing I must wear is love. Love is what binds us all together in perfect harmony. (Colossians 3:12–14)

Family and Ministry

Pause to lift up your family, your career, and your ministry before the Lord. Ask that you would have the privilege of sharing Christ with others and helping people grow in their knowledge of him.

Concerns for Others

There should be harmony among the members, so that all the members care for each other equally. If one part suffers, all the parts suffer with it, and if one part is honored, all the parts are glad. Now all of us together are Christ's body, and each one of us is a separate and necessary part of it. (1 Corinthians 12:25–27)

Missions

Intercede for national and world missions, and pray that those who have dedicated their lives to the fulfillment of the Great Commission will be strengthened, encouraged, and empowered.

Prayer of Thanksgiving

I will give thanks to the LORD and proclaim his greatness. May I let the whole world know what he has done. May I sing to him; yes, sing his praises and tell everyone about his miracles. (1 Chronicles 16:8–9)

I can be sure of this: The LORD has set apart the godly for himself. The LORD will answer when I call to him. (Psalm 4:3)

Pause to offer your own expressions of thanksgiving.

Concluding Prayer

May I trust in the LORD with all my heart; may I not depend on my own understanding but seek his will in all I do. He will direct my path. May I not be impressed with my own wisdom. Instead, may I fear the LORD and turn my back on evil. (Proverbs 3:5–7)

Day 14

Praise and Worship

Can you hold back the movements of the stars? Are you able to restrain the Pleiades or Orion? Can you ensure the proper sequence of the seasons or guide the constellation of the Bear with her cubs across the heavens? Do you know the laws of the universe and how God rules the earth? (Job 38:31–33)

I know that you can do anything, and no one can stop you. (Job 42:2)

Pause to express your thoughts of praise and worship.

Personal Examination

Remember that the temptations that come into your life are no different from what others experience. And God is faithful. He will keep the temptation from becoming so strong that you can't stand up against it. When you are tempted, he will show you a way out so that you will not give in to it. (1 Corinthians 10:13)

Ask the Spirit to search your heart and reveal any areas of unconfessed sin. Acknowledge these to the Lord and thank him for his forgiveness.

Commitment

May I run from anything that stimulates youthful lust and follow anything that makes me want to do right. May I pursue faith and love and peace, and enjoy the companionship of those who call on the Lord with pure hearts. (2 Timothy 2:22)

May I not get involved in foolish, ignorant arguments that only start fights. The Lord's servants must not quarrel but must be kind to everyone. They must be able to teach effectively and be patient with difficult people. (2 Timothy 2:23–24)

Pause to add your own prayers for commitment and renewal.

Personal Concerns

Here is my final conclusion: Fear God and obey his commands, for this is the duty of every person. God will judge us for everything we do, including every secret thing, whether good or bad. (Ecclesiastes 12:13–14)

Growth in Character

Pause to look to the Lord for the power to stand firm in the spiritual warfare against the world, the flesh, and spiritual forces of wickedness. Ask that you would grow in character and pursue the disciplines of the faith in a spirit of radical dependence upon him.

Concerns for Others

The godly know the rights of the poor; the wicked don't care to know. (Proverbs 29:7)

World Affairs

Lift up the needs of the poor and the hungry, the oppressed and the persecuted. Pray for those in positions of authority and ask for the blessings of peace rather than conflict.

Prayer of Thanksgiving

Every king in all the earth will give you thanks, O LORD, for all of them will hear your words. Yes, they will sing about the LORD's ways, for the glory of the LORD is very great. Though the LORD is great, he cares for the humble, but he keeps his distance from the proud. (Psalm 138:4–6)

Pause to offer your own expressions of thanksgiving.

Concluding Prayer

All honor to the God and Father of our Lord Jesus Christ, for it is by his boundless mercy that God has given us the privilege of being born again. Now we live with a wonderful expectation because Jesus Christ rose again from the dead. For God has reserved a priceless inheritance for his children. It is kept in heaven for you, pure and undefiled, beyond the reach of change and decay. (1 Peter 1:3–4)

In his kindness God called me to his eternal glory by means of Jesus Christ. After I have suffered a little while, he will restore, support, and strengthen me, and he will place me on a firm foundation. All power is his forever and ever. Amen. (1 Peter 5:10–11)

Day 15

Praise and Worship

We see Jesus, who "for a little while was made lower than the angels" and now is "crowned with glory and honor" because he suffered death for us. Yes, by God's grace, Jesus tasted death for everyone in all the world. And it was only right that God—who made everything and for whom everything was made—should bring his many children into glory. Through the suffering of Jesus, God made him a perfect leader, one fit to bring them into their salvation. (Hebrews 2:9–10)

You are the King of kings and Lord of lords. (Revelation 19:16)

Pause to express your thoughts of praise and worship.

Personal Examination

My destruction is sealed, for I am a sinful man and a member of a sinful race. Yet I have seen the King, the LORD Almighty! (Isaiah 6:5)

Ask the Spirit to search your heart and reveal any areas of unconfessed sin. Acknowledge these to the Lord and thank him for his forgiveness.

Commitment

When Uzziah had become powerful, he also became proud, which led to his downfall. He sinned against the

LORD his God by entering the sanctuary of the LORD's Temple and personally burning incense on the altar. (2 Chronicles 26:16)

When I am full and prosperous, that is the time to be careful. May I not become proud at that time and forget the LORD my God, who rescued me from slavery in the land of Egypt. He did it so I would never think that it was my own strength and energy that made me wealthy. (Deuteronomy 8:12–14, 17)

Pause to add your own prayers for commitment and renewal.

Personal Concerns

May I not spend the rest of my life chasing after evil desires, but be anxious to do the will of God. I have had enough in the past of the evil things that godless people enjoy—their immorality and lust, their feasting and drunkenness and wild parties, and their terrible worship of idols. (1 Peter 4:2–3)

Love and Compassion

Pause to ask for the grace of greater love and compassion for others. Pray that you will become a more Christlike person who considers the needs of others above your own, knowing that God is your provider and sustainer.

Concerns for Others

The harvest is so great, but the workers are few. Therefore, I will pray that the Lord who is in charge of the harvest will send out more workers for his fields. (Matthew 9:37–38; Luke 10:2)

Christian Witness

Pray on behalf of the people you personally know who have not yet entered into the joy of a personal relationship with Jesus. Intercede for your unsaved relatives, neighbors, co-workers, and friends.

Prayer of Thanksgiving

He is so rich in kindness that he purchased my freedom through the blood of his Son, and my sins are forgiven. He has showered his kindness on me, along with all wisdom and understanding. (Ephesians 1:7–8)

He raised me from the dead along with Christ, and I am seated with him in the heavenly realms—all because I am one with Christ Jesus. And so God can always point to me as an example of the incredible wealth of his favor and kindness toward me, as shown in all he has done for us through Christ Jesus. (Ephesians 2:6–7)

Pause to offer your own expressions of thanksgiving.

Concluding Prayer

Lord Jesus, all that the Father has given you will come to you, and you will never reject them. For you have come down from heaven to do the will of God who sent you, not to do what you want. And this is the will of God, that you should not lose even one of all those he has given you, but that you should raise them to eternal life at the last day. For it is your Father's will that all who see you and believe in you should have eternal life—that you should raise them at the last day. (John 6:37–40)

Day 16

Praise and Worship

The LORD, your Redeemer and Creator, says: "I am the LORD, who made all things. I alone stretched out the heavens. By myself I made the earth and everything in it." (Isaiah 44:24)

Blessing and glory and wisdom and thanksgiving and honor and power and strength belong to our God forever and forever. Amen! (Revelation 7:12)

Pause to express your thoughts of praise and worship.

Personal Examination

Haughtiness goes before destruction; humility precedes honor. (Proverbs 18:12)

Ask the Spirit to search your heart and reveal any areas of unconfessed sin. Acknowledge these to the Lord and thank him for his forgiveness.

Commitment

Follow my advice, my son; always treasure my commands. Obey them and live! Guard my teachings as your most precious possession. Tie them on your fingers as a reminder. Write them deep within your heart. Love wisdom like a sister; make insight a beloved member of your family. (Proverbs 7:1–4)

May I be careful to obey all the commands you give me; may I show love to the LORD my God by walking in his ways and clinging to him. (Deuteronomy 11:22)

Pause to add your own prayers for commitment and renewal.

Personal Concerns

May I test everything that is said and hold on to what is good. May I keep away from every kind of evil. (1 Thessalonians 5:21–22)

Faithfulness as a Steward

Pause to ask that God would empower you to become a more faithful and effective steward with all that he has entrusted to your care. Since he has given you a stewardship of talents, treasure, truth, time, and love and compassion, ask that you would use these gifts with fidelity in his service.

Concerns for Others

The LORD has said, "If my people who are called by my name will humble themselves and pray and seek my face and turn from their wicked ways, I will hear from heaven and will forgive their sins and heal their land." (2 Chronicles 7:14)

Government

Lift up those in local, state, and national government, and pray that those in positions of authority would look to God for wisdom in their decisions and practice.

Prayer of Thanksgiving

Your goodness is so great! You have stored up great blessings for those who honor you. You have done so much for those who come to you for protection, blessing them before the watching world. (Psalm 31:19)

God is my helper; The LORD is the one who keeps me alive. (Psalm 54:4)

Pause to offer your own expressions of thanksgiving.

Concluding Prayer

Can anything ever separate us from Christ's love? Does it mean he no longer loves us if we have trouble or calamity, or are persecuted, or are hungry or cold or in danger or threatened with death? (Even the Scriptures say, "For your sake we are killed every day; we are being slaughtered like sheep.") No, despite all these things, overwhelming victory is ours through Christ, who loved us. (Romans 8:35–37)

Day 17

Praise and Worship

The LORD is righteous in everything he does; he is filled with kindness. (Psalm 145:17)

Only you can tell me what is going to happen even before it happens. Everything you plan will come to pass, for you do whatever you wish. (Isaiah 46:10)

Pause to express your thoughts of praise and worship.

Personal Examination

Purify me from my sins, and I will be clean; wash me, and I will be whiter than snow. Oh, give me back my joy again; you have broken me—now let me rejoice. Don't keep looking at my sins. Remove the stain of my guilt. Create in me a clean heart, O God. Renew a right spirit within me. Do not banish me from your presence, and don't take your Holy Spirit from me. Restore to me again the joy of your salvation, and make me willing to obey you. Then I will teach your ways to sinners, and they will return to you. (Psalm 51:7–13)

Ask the Spirit to search your heart and reveal any areas of unconfessed sin. Acknowledge these to the Lord and thank him for his forgiveness.

Commitment

May I commit myself to instruction and attune my ears to hear words of knowledge. (Proverbs 23:12)

May I keep alert and pray. Otherwise temptation will overpower me. For though the spirit is willing enough, the body is weak! (Matthew 26:41)

Pause to add your own prayers for commitment and renewal.

Personal Concerns

O LORD, please hear my prayer! Listen to the prayers of those of us who delight in honoring you. Please grant me success now as I go to ask the king for a great favor. Put it into his heart to be kind to me. (Nehemiah 1:11)

Family and Ministry
Pause to lift up your family, your career, and your ministry before the Lord. Ask that you would have the privilege of sharing Christ with others and helping people grow in their knowledge of him.

Concerns for Others

So the Word became human and lived here on earth among us. He was full of unfailing love and faithfulness. And we have seen his glory, the glory of the only Son of the Father. (John 1:14)

Missions
Intercede for national and world missions, and pray that those who have dedicated their lives to the fulfillment of the

Great Commission will be strengthened, encouraged, and empowered.

Prayer of Thanksgiving

You are my God, and I will praise you! You are my God, and I will exalt you! Give thanks to the Lord, for he is good! His faithful love endures forever. (Psalm 118:28–29)

Pause to offer your own expressions of thanksgiving.

Concluding Prayer

Exult in his holy name; O worshipers of the Lord, rejoice! Search for the Lord and for his strength, and keep on searching. Think of the wonderful works he has done, the miracles, and the judgments he handed down. (1 Chronicles 16:10–12)

The Lord reigns forever, executing judgment from his throne. He will judge the world with justice and rule the nations with fairness. The Lord is a shelter for the oppressed, a refuge in times of trouble. Those who know your name trust in you, for you, O Lord, have never abandoned anyone who searches for you. (Psalm 9:7–10)

Day 18

Praise and Worship

How great you are, O Sovereign LORD! There is no one like you, and there is no other God. (2 Samuel 7:22)

You alone are the LORD. You made the skies and the heavens and all the stars. You made the earth and the seas and everything in them. You preserve and give life to everything, and all the angels of heaven worship you. (Nehemiah 9:6)

Pause to express your thoughts of praise and worship.

Personal Examination

I have swept away your sins like the morning mists. I have scattered your offenses like the clouds. Oh, return to me, for I have paid the price to set you free. (Isaiah 44:22)

Ask the Spirit to search your heart and reveal any areas of unconfessed sin. Acknowledge these to the Lord and thank him for his forgiveness.

Commitment

May I not treat your holy name as common and ordinary. I must treat you as holy, because it is you, the LORD, who makes me holy. (Leviticus 22:32)

The LORD is our God, the LORD alone. And I must love the LORD my God with all my heart, all my soul, and all my strength. (Deuteronomy 6:4–5)

Pause to add your own prayers for commitment and renewal.

Personal Concerns

May I spend my time and energy in training myself for spiritual fitness. Physical exercise has some value, but spiritual exercise is much more important, for it promises a reward in both this life and the next. (1 Timothy 4:7–8)

Growth in Character

Pause to look to the Lord for the power to stand firm in the spiritual warfare against the world, the flesh, and spiritual forces of wickedness. Ask that you would grow in character and pursue the disciplines of the faith in a spirit of radical dependence upon him.

Concerns for Others

Hear from heaven, where you live, and forgive. Give your people whatever they deserve, for you alone know the human heart. (2 Chronicles 6:30)

World Affairs

Lift up the needs of the poor and the hungry, the oppressed and the persecuted. Pray for those in positions of authority and ask for the blessings of peace rather than conflict.

Prayer of Thanksgiving

We thank you, O God! We give thanks because you are near. People everywhere tell of your mighty miracles. (Psalm 75:1)

Unfailing love and truth have met together. Righteousness and peace have kissed! Truth springs up from the earth, and righteousness smiles down from heaven. (Psalm 85:10–11)

Pause to offer your own expressions of thanksgiving.

Concluding Prayer

May the LORD our God show us his approval and make our efforts successful. Yes, make our efforts successful! (Psalm 90:17)

Day 19

Praise and Worship

O LORD, God of Israel, there is no God like you in all of heaven or earth. You keep your promises and show unfailing love to all who obey you and are eager to do your will. (1 Kings 8:23; 2 Chronicles 6:14)

I know that you alone are called the LORD, that you alone are the Most High, supreme over all the earth. (Psalm 83:18)

Pause to express your thoughts of praise and worship.

Personal Examination

The LORD sees clearly what a man does, examining every path he takes. (Proverbs 5:21)

Ask the Spirit to search your heart and reveal any areas of unconfessed sin. Acknowledge these to the Lord and thank him for his forgiveness.

Commitment

May I beware and not be greedy for what I don't have. Real life is not measured by how much we own. (Luke 12:15)

May I stay away from the love of money and be satisfied with what I have. For you have said, "I will never fail you. I will never forsake you." (Hebrews 13:5)

Pause to add your own prayers for commitment and renewal.

Personal Concerns

Turn to me and have mercy on me, for I am alone and in deep distress. My problems go from bad to worse. Oh, save me from them all! Feel my pain and see my trouble. Forgive all my sins. (Psalm 25:16–18)

Knowing, Loving, and Trusting God

Pause to ask God for the grace to know and please him. Ask him to enlarge your capacity to love him more and abide wholly in him.

Concerns for Others

We should not be drunk with wine, because that will ruin our life. Instead, let the Holy Spirit fill and control us. Then we will sing psalms and hymns and spiritual songs among ourselves, making music to the Lord in our hearts. And we will always give thanks for everything to God the Father in the name of our Lord Jesus Christ. (Ephesians 5:18–20)

Churches and Ministries

Ask God to work on behalf of the people and concerns at your local church. Pray for his blessing and power in the ministries that are engaged in Christian witness, discipleship, education, and those serving people in need.

Prayer of Thanksgiving

With all my heart I will praise you, O LORD my God. I will give glory to your name forever, for your love for me is very great. You have rescued me from the depths of death! (Psalm 86:12–13)

May all who are godly be happy in the LORD and praise his holy name! (Psalm 97:12)

Pause to offer your own expressions of thanksgiving.

Concluding Prayer

A single day in your courts is better than a thousand anywhere else! I would rather be a gatekeeper in the house of my God than live the good life in the homes of the wicked. For the LORD God is our light and protector. He gives us grace and glory. No good thing will the LORD withhold from those who do what is right. O LORD Almighty, happy are those who trust in you. (Psalm 84:10–12)

Day 20

Praise and Worship

Not to us, O LORD, but to you goes all the glory for your unfailing love and faithfulness. (Psalm 115:1)

Praise the LORD! How good it is to sing praises to our God! How delightful and how right! (Psalm 147:1)

Pause to express your thoughts of praise and worship.

Personal Examination

Even the depths of Death and Destruction are known by the LORD. How much more does he know the human heart! (Proverbs 15:11)

Ask the Spirit to search your heart and reveal any areas of unconfessed sin. Acknowledge these to the Lord and thank him for his forgiveness.

Commitment

May I come back to my God! I will act on the principles of love and justice, and always live in confident dependence on my God. (Hosea 12:6)

May I live on more than bread; I must feed on every word of God. (Matthew 4:4)

Pause to add your own prayers for commitment and renewal.

Personal Concerns

May I obey your laws and commands that you give and follow your instructions in every detail. (Deuteronomy 4:40; 5:32)

Greater Wisdom

Pause to ask God for the grace to develop an eternal perspective on your life and concerns, and that he would renew your mind with his truth. Ask for the power to order your steps with wisdom and skill in each area of life so that you will seek to please him rather than impress others.

Concerns for Others

We have a great High Priest who has gone to heaven, Jesus the Son of God. Let us cling to him and never stop trusting him. This High Priest of ours understands our weaknesses, for he faced all of the same temptations we do, yet he did not sin. So let us come boldly to the throne of our gracious God. There we will receive his mercy, and we will find grace to help us when we need it. (Hebrews 4:14–16)

Loved Ones

Lift up the members of your immediate family and your extended family. Pray for the spiritual, emotional, and physical concerns of your loved ones.

Prayer of Thanksgiving

I am the Lord your God, who rescued you from slavery. (Exodus 20:2)

Are you not the same today, the one who dried up the sea, making a path of escape when you saved your people? (Isaiah 51:10)

Pause to offer your own expressions of thanksgiving.

Concluding Prayer

You have sworn by your own name, and you will never go back on your word: Every knee will bow to you, and every tongue will confess allegiance to your name. (Isaiah 45:23)

You are worthy to take the scroll and break its seals and open it. For you were killed, and your blood has ransomed people for God from every tribe and language and people and nation. And you have caused them to become God's Kingdom and his priests. And they will reign on the earth. (Revelation 5:9–10)

Day 21

Praise and Worship

How great is the LORD, and how much we should praise him in the city of our God, which is on his holy mountain! O God, we meditate on your unfailing love as we worship in your Temple. As your name deserves, O God, you will be praised to the ends of the earth. Your strong right hand is filled with victory. (Psalm 48:1, 9–10)

Come, let us worship and bow down. Let us kneel before the LORD our maker. (Psalm 95:6)

Pause to express your thoughts of praise and worship.

Personal Examination

You look deep within the mind and heart, O righteous God. (Psalm 7:9)

The LORD's searchlight penetrates the human spirit, exposing every hidden motive. (Proverbs 20:27)

Ask the Spirit to search your heart and reveal any areas of unconfessed sin. Acknowledge these to the Lord and thank him for his forgiveness.

Commitment

Like Job, may I be blameless and upright, fearing God and shunning evil. (Job 1:1)

I will be careful to live a blameless life—when will you come to my aid? I will lead a life of integrity in my own home. I will refuse to look at anything vile and vulgar. I hate all crooked dealings; I will have nothing to do with them. (Psalm 101:2–3)

Pause to add your own prayers for commitment and renewal.

Personal Concerns

O God, listen to my cry! Hear my prayer! From the ends of the earth, I will cry to you for help, for my heart is overwhelmed. Lead me to the towering rock of safety, for you are my safe refuge, a fortress where my enemies cannot reach me. Let me live forever in your sanctuary, safe beneath the shelter of your wings! (Psalm 61:1–4)

Spiritual Insight

Pause to ask that the Holy Spirit would give you understanding and insight into the word of truth, so that you will have a growing grasp of your identity in Christ—where you came from, who you are, and where you are going. Ask for a clearer understanding of God's purpose for your life.

Concerns for Others

We know what real love is because Christ gave up his life for us. And so we also ought to give up our lives for our Christian brothers and sisters. But if anyone has enough money to live well and sees a brother or sister in need and refuses to help—how can God's love be in that person? Dear children, let us stop just saying we love each other; let us really show it by our actions. (1 John 3:16–18)

Other Believers

Intercede in the lives of your personal friends, and ask that the Lord will bless their families, their careers, and their ministries. Pray that he will comfort and strengthen those who are oppressed and in need.

Prayer of Thanksgiving

Listen! The LORD is not too weak to save you, and he is not becoming deaf. He can hear you when you call. But there is a problem—your sins have cut you off from God. Because of your sin, he has turned away and will not listen anymore. He was amazed to see that no one intervened to help the oppressed. So he himself stepped in to save them with his mighty power and justice. He put on righteousness as his body armor and placed the helmet of salvation on his head. He clothed himself with the robes of vengeance and godly fury. He will repay his enemies for their evil deeds. His fury will fall on his foes in distant lands. Then at last they will respect and glorify the name of the LORD throughout the world. For he will come like a flood tide driven by the breath of the LORD. (Isaiah 59:1–2, 16–19)

Pause to offer your own expressions of thanksgiving.

Concluding Prayer

LORD, my heart is not proud; my eyes are not haughty. I don't concern myself with matters too great or awesome for me. But I have stilled and quieted myself, just as a small child is quiet with its mother. Yes, like a small child is my soul within me. (Psalm 131:1–2)

Day 22

Praise and Worship

Let the godly sing with joy to the Lord, for it is fitting to praise him. (Psalm 33:1)

Lord, we love to obey your laws; our heart's desire is to glorify your name. (Isaiah 26:8)

Pause to express your thoughts of praise and worship.

Personal Examination

Come, let us return to the Lord! He has torn us in pieces; now he will heal us. He has injured us; now he will bandage our wounds. In just a short time, he will restore us so we can live in his presence. (Hosea 6:1–2)

Ask the Spirit to search your heart and reveal any areas of unconfessed sin. Acknowledge these to the Lord and thank him for his forgiveness.

Commitment

May I have no sexual immorality, impurity, or greed in me. Such sins have no place among God's people. Obscene stories, foolish talk, and coarse jokes—these are not for me. Instead, let me be thankful to God. (Ephesians 5:3–4)

May I fix my thoughts on what is true and honorable and right. May I think about things that are pure and lovely and admirable, things that are excellent and worthy of praise. I will keep putting into practice all I have learned, and the God of peace will be with me. (Philippians 4:8–9)

Pause to add your own prayers for commitment and renewal.

Personal Concerns

May I be strong and courageous, for my work will be rewarded. (2 Chronicles 15:7)

Love and Compassion

Pause to ask for the grace of greater love and compassion for others. Pray that you will become a more Christlike person who considers the needs of others above your own, knowing that God is your provider and sustainer.

Concerns for Others

May the LORD make my love grow and overflow to other Christians and unbelievers. (1 Thessalonians 3:12)

Christian Witness

Pray on behalf of the people you personally know who have not yet entered into the joy of a personal relationship with Jesus. Intercede for your unsaved relatives, neighbors, co-workers, and friends.

Prayer of Thanksgiving

I will sing out my thanks to the LORD! Praise the LORD! For though I was poor and needy, he delivered me from my oppressors. (Jeremiah 20:13)

The LORD is good. When trouble comes, he is a strong refuge. And he knows everyone who trusts in him. (Nahum 1:7)

Pause to offer your own expressions of thanksgiving.

Concluding Prayer

I lie awake thinking of you, meditating on you through the night. I think how much you have helped me; I sing for joy in the shadow of your protecting wings. I follow close behind you; your strong right hand holds me securely. (Psalm 63:6–8)

Day 23

Praise and Worship

Shout joyful praises to God, all the earth! Sing about the glory of his name! Tell the world how glorious he is. Say to God, "How awesome are your deeds! Your enemies cringe before your mighty power. Everything on earth will worship you; they will sing your praises, shouting your name in glorious songs." (Psalm 66:1–4)

I can never stop praising you; I declare your glory all day long. (Psalm 71:8)

Pause to express your thoughts of praise and worship.

Personal Examination

The LORD is good and does what is right; he shows the proper path to those who go astray. He leads the humble in what is right, teaching them his way. (Psalm 25:8–9)

Ask the Spirit to search your heart and reveal any areas of unconfessed sin. Acknowledge these to the Lord and thank him for his forgiveness.

Commitment

May I love the LORD my God with all my heart and soul, and worship him. (Deuteronomy 11:13)

May I take it to heart to honor your name. (Malachi 2:2)

May I worship the Lord my God, and serve him only. (Matthew 4:10)

Pause to add your own prayers for commitment and renewal.

Personal Concerns

So look at us as mere servants of Christ who have been put in charge of explaining God's secrets. Now, a person who is put in charge as a manager must be faithful. (1 Corinthians 4:1–2)

Faithfulness as a Steward
Pause to ask that God would empower you to become a more faithful and effective steward with all that he has entrusted to your care. Since he has given you a stewardship of talents, treasure, truth, time, and love and compassion, ask that you would use these gifts with fidelity in his service.

Concerns for Others

We have sinned terribly by not obeying the commands, laws, and regulations that you gave us through your servant Moses. (Nehemiah 1:7)

Government
Lift up those in local, state, and national government, and pray that those in positions of authority would look to God for wisdom in their decisions and practice.

Prayer of Thanksgiving

Praise the LORD, I tell myself; with my whole heart, I will praise his holy name. Praise the LORD, I tell myself, and never forget the good things he does for me. He forgives all my sins and heals all my diseases. He ransoms me from death and surrounds me with love and tender mercies. He fills my life with good things. My youth is renewed like the eagle's! (Psalm 103:1–5)

Pause to offer your own expressions of thanksgiving.

Concluding Prayer

I will be silent, and know that you are God! You will be honored by every nation. You will be honored throughout the world. (Psalm 46:10)

Bless the LORD, the God of Israel, who lives forever from eternal ages past. Amen and amen! (Psalm 41:13)

Day 24

Praise and Worship

You made all the delicate, inner parts of my body and knit me together in my mother's womb. Thank you for making me so wonderfully complex! Your workmanship is marvelous—and how well I know it. You watched me as I was being formed in utter seclusion, as I was woven together in the dark of the womb. You saw me before I was born. Every day of my life was recorded in your book. Every moment was laid out before a single day had passed. (Psalm 139:13–16)

Pause to express your thoughts of praise and worship.

Personal Examination

From within, out of a person's heart, come evil thoughts, sexual immorality, theft, murder, adultery, greed, wickedness, deceit, eagerness for lustful pleasure, envy, slander, pride, and foolishness. All these vile things come from within; they are what defile you and make you unacceptable to God. (Mark 7:21–23)

Ask the Spirit to search your heart and reveal any areas of unconfessed sin. Acknowledge these to the Lord and thank him for his forgiveness.

Commitment

Teach me to do your will, for you are my God. May your gracious Spirit lead me forward on a firm footing. (Psalm 143:10)

May I get all the advice and instruction I can, and be wise the rest of my life. (Proverbs 19:20)

Pause to add your own prayers for commitment and renewal.

Personal Concerns

May I get rid of anger, rage, malicious behavior, slander, and dirty language. (Colossians 3:8)

Family and Ministry

Pause to lift up your family, your career, and your ministry before the Lord. Ask that you would have the privilege of sharing Christ with others and helping people grow in their knowledge of him.

Concerns for Others

My dear brothers and sisters, be strong and steady, always enthusiastic about the Lord's work, for you know that nothing you do for the Lord is ever useless. (1 Corinthians 15:58)

Missions

Intercede for national and world missions, and pray that those who have dedicated their lives to the fulfillment of the Great Commission will be strengthened, encouraged, and empowered.

Prayer of Thanksgiving

LORD, you said, "Let bright lights appear in the sky to separate the day from the night. They will be signs to mark off the seasons, the days, and the years. Let their light shine down upon the earth." And so it was. For you made two great lights, the sun and the moon, to shine down upon the earth. The greater one, the sun, presides during the day; the lesser one, the moon, presides through the night. You also made the stars. You set these lights in the heavens to light the earth, to govern the day and the night, and to separate the light from the darkness. And you saw that it was good. (Genesis 1:14–18)

You are the one who made the earth and created people to live on it. With your hands you stretched out the heavens. All the millions of stars are at your command. (Isaiah 45:12)

Pause to offer your own expressions of thanksgiving.

Concluding Prayer

Your word is a lamp for my feet and a light for my path. I am determined to keep your principles, even forever, to the very end. (Psalm 119:105, 112)

Day 25

Praise and Worship

I will praise you, my God and King, and bless your name forever and ever. I will bless you every day, and I will praise you forever. Great is the LORD! He is most worthy of praise! His greatness is beyond discovery! (Psalm 145:1–3)

Golden splendor comes from the mountain of God. He is clothed in dazzling splendor. We cannot imagine the power of the Almighty, yet he is so just and merciful that he does not oppress us. (Job 37:22–23)

Pause to express your thoughts of praise and worship.

Personal Examination

The LORD your God is gracious and merciful. If you return to him, he will not continue to turn his face from you. (2 Chronicles 30:9)

Ask the Spirit to search your heart and reveal any areas of unconfessed sin. Acknowledge these to the Lord and thank him for his forgiveness.

Commitment

If I stay joined to you and your words remain in me, I may ask any request I like, and it will be granted! As

I ask, using your name, I will receive, and I will have abundant joy. (John 15:7; 16:24)

May I live according to my new life in the Holy Spirit. Then I won't be doing what my flesh craves. The old flesh loves to do evil, which is just opposite from what the Holy Spirit wants. And the Spirit gives me desires that are opposite from what the flesh desires. These two forces are constantly fighting each other, and my choices are never free from this conflict. But when I am directed by the Holy Spirit, I am no longer subject to the law. (Galatians 5:16–18)

Pause to add your own prayers for commitment and renewal.

Personal Concerns

I pray to you, O LORD. I say, "You are my place of refuge. You are all I really want in life." (Psalm 142:5)

Growth in Character
Pause to look to the Lord for the power to stand firm in the spiritual warfare against the world, the flesh, and spiritual forces of wickedness. Ask that you would grow in character and pursue the disciplines of the faith in a spirit of radical dependence upon him.

Concerns for Others

Many people say, "Who will show us better times?" Let the smile of your face shine on us, LORD. (Psalm 4:6)

World Affairs

Lift up the needs of the poor and the hungry, the oppressed and the persecuted. Pray for those in positions of authority and ask for the blessings of peace rather than conflict.

Prayer of Thanksgiving

O LORD my God, you have done many miracles for us. Your plans for us are too numerous to list. If I tried to recite all your wonderful deeds, I would never come to the end of them. (Psalm 40:5)

I will praise you forever, O God, for what you have done. I will wait for your mercies in the presence of your people. (Psalm 52:9)

Pause to offer your own expressions of thanksgiving.

Concluding Prayer

Christ is the visible image of the invisible God. He existed before God made anything at all and is supreme over all creation. Christ is the one through whom God created everything in heaven and earth. He made the things we can see and the things we can't see—kings, kingdoms, rulers, and authorities. Everything has been created through him and for him. He existed before everything else began, and he holds all creation together. (Colossians 1:15–17)

The highest heavens and the earth and everything in it all belong to the LORD your God. (Deuteronomy 10:14)

Day 26

Praise and Worship

True wisdom and power are with you; counsel and understanding are yours. (Job 12:13)

You are holy; The praises of Israel surround your throne. (Psalm 22:3)

Pause to express your thoughts of praise and worship.

Personal Examination

Oh, what joy for those whose rebellion is forgiven, whose sin is put out of sight! Yes, what joy for those whose record the LORD has cleared of sin, whose lives are lived in complete honesty! When I refused to confess my sin, I was weak and miserable, and I groaned all day long. Day and night your hand of discipline was heavy on me. My strength evaporated like water in the summer heat. Finally, I confessed all my sins to you and stopped trying to hide them. I said to myself, "I will confess my rebellion to the LORD." And you forgave me! All my guilt is gone. (Psalm 32:1–5)

Ask the Spirit to search your heart and reveal any areas of unconfessed sin. Acknowledge these to the Lord and thank him for his forgiveness.

Commitment

May I have a sincere love for others because I was cleansed from my sins when I accepted the truth of the Good News. May I really love others intensely with all my heart. (1 Peter 1:22)

Pause to add your own prayers for commitment and renewal.

Personal Concerns

You slaves must obey your earthly masters in everything you do. Try to please them all the time, not just when they are watching you. Obey them willingly because of your reverent fear of the Lord. Work hard and cheerfully at whatever you do, as though you were working for the Lord rather than for people. Remember that the Lord will give you an inheritance as your reward, and the Master you are serving is Christ. (Colossians 3:22–24)

Knowing, Loving, and Trusting God

Pause to ask God for the grace to know and please him. Ask him to enlarge your capacity to love him more and abide wholly in him.

Concerns for Others

We are all one body, we have the same Spirit, and we have all been called to the same glorious future. There is only one Lord, one faith, one baptism, and there is only one God and Father, who is over us all and in us all and living through us all. (Ephesians 4:4–6)

Churches and Ministries

Ask God to work on behalf of the people and concerns at your local church. Pray for his blessing and power in the ministries that are engaged in Christian witness, discipleship, education, and those serving people in need.

Prayer of Thanksgiving

LORD, you said, "Let us make people in our image, to be like ourselves. They will be masters over all life—the fish in the sea, the birds in the sky, and all the livestock, wild animals, and small animals." So you created people in your own image; you patterned them after yourself; male and female you created them. You blessed them and told them, "Multiply and fill the earth and subdue it. Be masters over the fish and birds and all the animals." And you said, "Look! I have given you the seed-bearing plants throughout the earth and all the fruit trees for your food. And I have given all the grasses and other green plants to the animals and birds for their food." And so it was. Then you looked over all you had made, and saw that it was excellent in every way. (Genesis 1:26–31)

Pause to offer your own expressions of thanksgiving.

Concluding Prayer

There is no condemnation for those who belong to Christ Jesus. For the power of the life-giving Spirit has freed me through Christ Jesus from the power of sin that leads to death. (Romans 8:1–2)

Day 27

Praise and Worship

You are the LORD; you do not change. (Malachi 3:6)

God is light and there is no darkness in him at all. (1 John 1:5)

Fear God and give him glory, for the time has come when he will sit as judge. Worship him who made heaven and earth, the sea, and all the springs of water. (Revelation 14:7)

Pause to express your thoughts of praise and worship.

Personal Examination

The LORD leads with unfailing love and faithfulness all those who keep his covenant and obey his decrees. For the honor of your name, O LORD, forgive my many, many sins. (Psalm 25:10–11)

Ask the Spirit to search your heart and reveal any areas of unconfessed sin. Acknowledge these to the Lord and thank him for his forgiveness.

Commitment

May I be decent and true in everything I do, so that everyone can approve of my behavior. I will not participate in wild parties and getting drunk, or in adultery and immoral living, or in fighting and jealousy. Instead, I will let the Lord Jesus Christ take control of me and not think of ways to indulge my evil desires. (Romans 13:13–14)

Because I have these promises, let me cleanse myself from everything that can defile my body or spirit. And let me work toward complete purity because I fear God. (2 Corinthians 7:1)

Pause to add your own prayers for commitment and renewal.

Personal Concerns

May I not nurse hatred in my heart for any of my relatives. I will confront my neighbors directly so I will not be held guilty for their crimes. (Leviticus 19:17)

May I never seek revenge or bear a grudge against anyone, but love my neighbor as myself. (Leviticus 19:18)

Greater Wisdom
Pause to ask God for the grace to develop an eternal perspective on your life and concerns, and that he would renew your mind with his truth. Ask for the power to order your steps with wisdom and skill in each area of life so that you will seek to please him rather than impress others.

Concerns for Others

I will certainly not sin against the LORD by ending my prayers for you. (1 Samuel 12:23)

Loved Ones

Lift up the members of your immediate family and your extended family. Pray for the spiritual, emotional, and physical concerns of your loved ones.

Prayer of Thanksgiving

Always be full of joy in the Lord. I say it again—rejoice! (Philippians 4:4)

I have been appointed by the command of God our Savior and Christ Jesus who is my hope. (1 Timothy 1:1)

Pause to offer your own expressions of thanksgiving.

Concluding Prayer

This is what the LORD says: "Let not the wise man gloat in his wisdom, or the mighty man in his might, or the rich man in his riches. Let them boast in this alone: that they truly know me and understand that I am the LORD who is just and righteous, whose love is unfailing, and that I delight in these things. I, the LORD, have spoken!" (Jeremiah 9:23–24)

I say to myself, "The LORD is my inheritance; therefore, I will hope in him!" The LORD is wonderfully good to those who wait for him and seek him. So it is good to wait quietly for salvation from the LORD. (Lamentations 3:24–26)

Day 28

Praise and Worship

The LORD stretched out the heavens, laid the foundations of the earth, and formed the spirit within humans. (Zechariah 12:1)

You are the LORD, the God of the spirits of all living things. (Numbers 27:16)

Nothing is too hard for the LORD. (Genesis 18:14)

Pause to express your thoughts of praise and worship.

Personal Examination

I have sinned against the LORD, the God of Israel. (Joshua 7:20)

Ask the Spirit to search your heart and reveal any areas of unconfessed sin. Acknowledge these to the Lord and thank him for his forgiveness.

Commitment

Teach me to make the most of my time, so that I may grow in wisdom. (Psalm 90:12)

May I look straight ahead, and fix my eyes on what lies before me. May I mark out a straight path for my feet; then stick to the path and stay safe. May I not get sidetracked; keeping my feet from following evil. (Proverbs 4:25–27)

Pause to add your own prayers for commitment and renewal.

Personal Concerns

May I never say "God is tempting me." God is never tempted to do wrong, and he never tempts anyone else either. Temptation comes from the lure of our own evil desires. These evil desires lead to evil actions, and evil actions lead to death. (James 1:13–15)

Spiritual Insight

Pause to ask that the Holy Spirit would give you understanding and insight into the word of truth, so that you will have a growing grasp of your identity in Christ—where you came from, who you are, and where you are going. Ask for a clearer understanding of God's purpose for your life.

Concerns for Others

Continue to love each other with true Christian love. Don't forget to show hospitality to strangers, for some who have done this have entertained angels without realizing it! Don't forget about those in prison. Suffer with them as though you were there yourself. Share the sorrow of those being mistreated, as though you feel their pain in your own bodies. (Hebrews 13:1–3)

Other Believers

Intercede in the lives of your personal friends, and ask that the Lord will bless their families, their careers, and their ministries. Pray that he will comfort and strengthen those who are oppressed and in need.

Prayer of Thanksgiving

Give thanks to the LORD and proclaim his greatness. Let the whole world know what he has done. Sing to him; yes, sing his praises. Tell everyone about his miracles. Exult in his holy name; O worshipers of the LORD, rejoice! (Psalm 105:1–3)

Pause to offer your own expressions of thanksgiving.

Concluding Prayer

Through each day the LORD pours his unfailing love upon me, and through each night I sing his songs, praying to God who gives me life. (Psalm 42:8)

Bless the LORD God, the God of Israel, who alone does such wonderful things. Bless his glorious name forever! Let the whole earth be filled with his glory. Amen and amen! (Psalm 72:18–19)

Day 29

Praise and Worship

I can never escape from your spirit! I can never get away from your presence! If I go up to heaven, you are there; if I go down to the place of the dead, you are there. If I ride the wings of the morning, if I dwell by the farthest oceans, even there your hand will guide me, and your strength will support me. I could ask the darkness to hide me and the light around me to become night—but even in darkness I cannot hide from you. To you the night shines as bright as day. Darkness and light are both alike to you. (Psalm 139:7–12)

Pause to express your thoughts of praise and worship.

Personal Examination

People may think they are doing what is right, but the LORD examines the heart. (Proverbs 21:2)

Ask the Spirit to search your heart and reveal any areas of unconfessed sin. Acknowledge these to the Lord and thank him for his forgiveness.

Commitment

May I never exchange my God, the glorious God, for worthless idols! I will never forsake you—the fountain of living water. (Jeremiah 2:11, 13)

Pause to add your own prayers for commitment and renewal.

Personal Concerns

When I am afraid, I put my trust in you. O God, I praise your word. I trust in God, so why should I be afraid? What can mere mortals do to me? (Psalm 56:3–4)

Love and Compassion

Pause to ask for the grace of greater love and compassion for others. Pray that you will become a more Christlike person who considers the needs of others above your own, knowing that God is your provider and sustainer.

Concerns for Others

Those who become Christians become new persons. They are not the same anymore, for the old life is gone. A new life has begun.

All this newness of life is from God, who brought us back to himself through what Christ did. And God has given us the task of reconciling people to him. For God was in Christ, reconciling the world to himself, no longer counting people's sins against them. This is the wonderful message he has given us to tell others. (2 Corinthians 5:17–19)

Christian Witness

Pray on behalf of the people you personally know who have not yet entered into the joy of a personal relationship with Jesus. Intercede for your unsaved relatives, neighbors, co-workers, and friends.

Prayer of Thanksgiving

Praise the LORD! I will thank the LORD with all my heart as I meet with his godly people. How amazing are the deeds of the LORD! All who delight in him should ponder them. Everything he does reveals his glory and majesty. His righteousness never fails. Who can forget the wonders he performs? How gracious and merciful is our LORD! (Psalm 111:1–4)

Pause to offer your own expressions of thanksgiving.

Concluding Prayer

If anyone wants to be your follower, he must put aside selfish ambition, shoulder his cross, and follow you. If we try to keep our life for ourselves, we will lose it. But if we give up our life for you, we will find true life. How do we benefit if we gain the whole world but lose our own soul in the process? Is anything worth more than a soul? (Matthew 16:24–26; Mark 8:34–37; Luke 9:23–25)

I will know the truth, and the truth will set me free. Everyone who sins is a slave of sin. A slave is not a permanent member of the family, but a son is part of the family forever. So if the Son sets me free, I will indeed be free. (John 8:32, 34–36)

Day 30

Praise and Worship

The LORD is king! He is robed in majesty. Indeed, the LORD is robed in majesty and armed with strength. The world is firmly established; it cannot be shaken. Your throne, O LORD, has been established from time immemorial. You yourself are from the everlasting past. Your royal decrees cannot be changed. The nature of your reign, O LORD, is holiness forever. (Psalm 93:1–2, 5)

Praise the LORD, I tell myself; O LORD my God, how great you are! You are robed with honor and with majesty. (Psalm 104:1)

Pause to express your thoughts of praise and worship.

Personal Examination

The human heart is most deceitful and desperately wicked. Who really knows how bad it is? But I know! I, the LORD, search all hearts and examine secret motives. I give all people their due rewards, according to what their actions deserve. (Jeremiah 17:9–10)

Ask the Spirit to search your heart and reveal any areas of unconfessed sin. Acknowledge these to the Lord and thank him for his forgiveness.

Commitment

May I be strong with the Lord's mighty power as I put on all of God's armor so that I will be able to stand firm against all strategies and tricks of the Devil. (Ephesians 6:10–11)

Because I live in the light, let me think clearly, protected by the body armor of faith and love, and wearing as our helmet the confidence of our salvation. (1 Thessalonians 5:8)

Pause to add your own prayers for commitment and renewal.

Personal Concerns

You know how full of love and kindness our Lord Jesus Christ was. Though he was very rich, yet for your sakes he became poor, so that by his poverty he could make you rich. (2 Corinthians 8:9)

Faithfulness as a Steward

Pause to ask that God would empower you to become a more faithful and effective steward with all that he has entrusted to your care. Since he has given you a stewardship of talents, treasure, truth, time, and love and compassion, ask that you would use these gifts with fidelity in his service.

Concerns for Others

Godliness exalts a nation, but sin is a disgrace to any people. (Proverbs 14:34)

Government

Lift up those in local, state, and national government, and pray that those in positions of authority would look to God for wisdom in their decisions and practice.

Prayer of Thanksgiving

But I trust in your unfailing love. I will rejoice because you have rescued me. I will sing to the LORD because he has been so good to me. (Psalm 13:5–6)

Praise the LORD! For he has heard my cry for mercy. The LORD is my strength, my shield from every danger. I trust in him with all my heart. He helps me, and my heart is filled with joy. I burst out in songs of thanksgiving. (Psalm 28:6–7)

Pause to offer your own expressions of thanksgiving.

Concluding Prayer

Without question, this is the great mystery of our faith: Christ appeared in the flesh and was shown to be righteous by the Spirit. He was seen by angels and was announced to the nations. He was believed on in the world and was taken up into heaven. (1 Timothy 3:16)

Day 31

Praise and Worship

"To whom will you compare me? Who is my equal?" asks the Holy One. Look up into the heavens. Who created all the stars? You bring them out one after another, calling each by its name. And you count them to see that none are lost or have strayed away. Don't we know that the LORD is the everlasting God, the Creator of all the earth? You never grow faint or weary. No one can measure the depths of your understanding. (Isaiah 40:25–26, 28)

LORD, you remain the same forever! Your throne continues from generation to generation. (Lamentations 5:19)

Pause to express your thoughts of praise and worship.

Personal Examination

If we are defeated by our enemies because we have sinned against you, and if we turn to you and call on your name and pray to you, then you will hear from heaven and forgive our sins. Hear from heaven and forgive the sins of your servants, your people. Teach us to do what is right, and send rain on your land that you have given to us. If we sin against you—and who has never sinned?—you may become angry with us and let our enemies conquer us. May we turn to you with our whole heart and soul and pray. (1 Kings 8:33–34, 36, 46, 48)

Ask the Spirit to search your heart and reveal any areas of unconfessed sin. Acknowledge these to the Lord and thank him for his forgiveness.

Commitment

May I fear the glorious and awesome name—the Lord my God. (Deuteronomy 28:58)

May I serve the Lord with reverent fear and rejoice with trembling. (Psalm 2:11)

May I give you my heart. May my eyes delight in your ways of wisdom. (Proverbs 23:26)

Pause to add your own prayers for commitment and renewal.

Personal Concerns

I am praying to you because I know you will answer, O God. Bend down and listen as I pray. Show me your unfailing love in wonderful ways. You save with your strength those who seek refuge from their enemies. Guard me as the apple of your eye. Hide me in the shadow of your wings. (Psalm 17:6–8)

Family and Ministry

Pause to lift up your family, your career, and your ministry before the Lord. Ask that you would have the privilege of sharing Christ with others and helping people grow in their knowledge of him.

Concerns for Others

I want for you to receive a well-earned reward because of your kindness. (Philippians 4:17)

Missions

Intercede for national and world missions, and pray that those who have dedicated their lives to the fulfillment of the Great Commission will be strengthened, encouraged, and empowered.

Prayer of Thanksgiving

The LORD saves the godly; he is their fortress in times of trouble. The LORD helps them, rescuing them from the wicked. He saves them, and they find shelter in him. (Psalm 37:39–40)

Pause to offer your own expressions of thanksgiving.

Concluding Prayer

For a child is born to us, a son is given to us. And the government will rest on his shoulders. These will be his royal titles: Wonderful Counselor, Mighty God, Everlasting Father, Prince of Peace. His ever expanding, peaceful government will never end. He will rule forever with fairness and justice from the throne of his ancestor David. The passionate commitment of the LORD Almighty will guarantee this! (Isaiah 9:6–7)

The Third Month

Day 1

Praise and Worship

O LORD, our LORD, the majesty of your name fills the earth! Your glory is higher than the heavens! (Psalm 8:1)

Great and marvelous are your actions, Lord God Almighty. Just and true are your ways, O King of the nations. Who will not fear, O Lord, and glorify your name? For you alone are holy. All nations will come and worship before you, for your righteous deeds have been revealed. (Revelation 15:3–4)

Pause to express your thoughts of praise and worship.

Personal Examination

He made our hearts, so he understands everything we do. (Psalm 33:15)

Ask the Spirit to search your heart and reveal any areas of unconfessed sin. Acknowledge these to the Lord and thank him for his forgiveness.

Commitment

Fear the LORD and judge with care, for the LORD our God does not tolerate perverted justice, partiality, or the taking of bribes. (2 Chronicles 19:7)

I will study your commandments and reflect on your ways. I will delight in your principles and not forget your word. Be good to your servant, that I may live and obey your word. Open my eyes to see the wonderful truths in your law. (Psalm 119:15–18)

Pause to add your own prayers for commitment and renewal.

Personal Concerns

May I not do as the wicked do or follow the path of evildoers. (Proverbs 4:14)

Growth in Character
Pause to look to the Lord for the power to stand firm in the spiritual warfare against the world, the flesh, and spiritual forces of wickedness. Ask that you would grow in character and pursue the disciplines of the faith in a spirit of radical dependence upon him.

Concerns for Others

Christ is the one through whom God created everything in heaven and earth. He made the things we can see and the things we can't see—kings, kingdoms, rulers, and authorities. Everything has been created through him and for him. He existed before everything else began, and he holds all creation together. (Colossians 1:16–17)

World Affairs
Lift up the needs of the poor and the hungry, the oppressed and the persecuted. Pray for those in positions of authority and ask for the blessings of peace rather than conflict.

Prayer of Thanksgiving

I will sing of the tender mercies of the LORD forever! Young and old will hear of your faithfulness. Your unfailing love will last forever. Your faithfulness is as enduring as the heavens. All heaven will praise your miracles, LORD; myriads of angels will praise you for your faithfulness. For who in all of heaven can compare with the LORD? What mightiest angel is anything like the LORD? The highest angelic powers stand in awe of God. He is far more awesome than those who surround his throne. LORD God Almighty! Where is there anyone as mighty as you, LORD? Faithfulness is your very character. (Psalm 89:1–2, 5–8)

Pause to offer your own expressions of thanksgiving.

Concluding Prayer

I am the living bread that came down out of heaven. Anyone who eats this bread will live forever; this bread is my flesh, offered so the world may live. (John 6:51)

You are the light of the world. If I follow you, I won't be stumbling through the darkness, because I will have the light that leads to life. (John 8:12)

Day 2

Praise and Worship

O LORD, what great miracles you do! And how deep are your thoughts. Only an ignorant person would not know this! Only a fool would not understand it. Although the wicked flourish like weeds, and evildoers blossom with success, there is only eternal destruction ahead of them. But you are exalted in the heavens. You, O LORD, continue forever. (Psalm 92:5–8)

You are the LORD; that is your name! You will not give your glory to anyone else. You will not share your praise with carved idols. (Isaiah 42:8)

Pause to express your thoughts of praise and worship.

Personal Examination

But the LORD is in his holy Temple; the LORD still rules from heaven. He watches everything closely, examining everyone on earth. (Psalm 11:4)

Ask the Spirit to search your heart and reveal any areas of unconfessed sin. Acknowledge these to the Lord and thank him for his forgiveness.

Commitment

Jesus prayed: "O Father, Lord of heaven and earth, thank you for hiding the truth from those who think themselves so wise and clever, and for revealing it to the childlike. Yes, Father, it pleased you to do it this way! My Father has given me authority over everything. No one really knows the Son except the Father, and no one really knows the Father except the Son and those to whom the Son chooses to reveal him." (Matthew 11:25–27; Luke 10:21–22)

This "foolish" plan of God is far wiser than the wisest of human plans, and God's weakness is far stronger than the greatest of human strength. God deliberately chose things the world considers foolish in order to shame those who think they are wise. And he chose those who are powerless to shame those who are powerful. God chose things despised by the world, things counted as nothing at all, and used them to bring to nothing what the world considers important, so that no one can ever boast in the presence of God. (1 Corinthians 1:25, 27–29)

Pause to add your own prayers for commitment and renewal.

Personal Concerns

May I be strong and courageous and do the work. May I not be afraid or discouraged, for the Lord, my God, is with me. He will not fail me or forsake me. (1 Chronicles 28:20)

Knowing, Loving, and Trusting God

Pause to ask God for the grace to know and please him. Ask him to enlarge your capacity to love him more and abide wholly in him.

Concerns for Others

Be sure that you feed and shepherd God's flock—his church, purchased with his blood—over whom the Holy Spirit has appointed you as elders. (Acts 20:28)

Churches and Ministries

Ask God to work on behalf of the people and concerns at your local church. Pray for his blessing and power in the ministries that are engaged in Christian witness, discipleship, education, and those serving people in need.

Prayer of Thanksgiving

I will rejoice in the LORD! I will be joyful in the God of my salvation. The Sovereign LORD is my strength! He will make me as surefooted as a deer and bring me safely over the mountains. (Habakkuk 3:18–19)

Pause to offer your own expressions of thanksgiving.

Concluding Prayer

You are the gate. Those who come in through you will be saved. Wherever they go, they will find green pastures. The thief's purpose is to steal and kill and destroy. Your purpose is to give life in all its fullness. (John 10:9–10)

Your sheep recognize your voice; you know them, and they follow you. You give them eternal life, and they will never perish. No one will snatch them away from you, for your Father has given them to you, and he is more powerful than anyone else. So no one can take them from you. You and the Father are one. (John 10:27–30)

Day 3

Praise and Worship

For the LORD Most High is awesome. He is the great King of all the earth. For God is the King over all the earth. Praise him with a psalm! God reigns above the nations, sitting on his holy throne. (Psalm 47:2, 7–8)

You must be treated as holy among those who are near you. You will be glorified before all the people. (Leviticus 10:3)

Pause to express your thoughts of praise and worship.

Personal Examination

O God, you take no pleasure in wickedness; you cannot tolerate the slightest sin. (Psalm 5:4)

Ask the Spirit to search your heart and reveal any areas of unconfessed sin. Acknowledge these to the Lord and thank him for his forgiveness.

Commitment

May I not worry about anything; instead, pray about everything. I will tell God what I need, and thank him for all he has done. If I do this, I will experience God's peace, which is far more wonderful than the human mind can understand. His peace will guard my heart and mind as I live in Christ Jesus. (Philippians 4:6–7)

May I think clearly and exercise self-control. I look forward to the special blessings that will come to me at the return of Jesus Christ. (1 Peter 1:13)

Pause to add your own prayers for commitment and renewal.

Personal Concerns

May I obey those who are in authority over me with deep respect and fear. I will serve them sincerely as I would serve Christ. I will work hard, but not just to please my masters when they are watching. As a slave of Christ, may I do the will of God with all my heart and work with enthusiasm, as though I were working for the Lord rather than for people. I remember that the Lord will reward each one of us for the good we do, whether we are slaves or free. (Ephesians 6:5–8)

Greater Wisdom

Pause to ask God for the grace to develop an eternal perspective on your life and concerns, and that he would renew your mind with his truth. Ask for the power to order your steps with wisdom and skill in each area of life so that you will seek to please him rather than impress others.

Concerns for Others

May we rejoice, change our ways, encourage each other, live in harmony and peace. Then the God of love and peace will be with us. (2 Corinthians 13:11)

Loved Ones

Lift up the members of your immediate family and your extended family. Pray for the spiritual, emotional, and physical concerns of your loved ones.

Prayer of Thanksgiving

Rejoice greatly, O people of Zion! Shout in triumph, O people of Jerusalem! Look, your king is coming to you. He is righteous and victorious, yet he is humble, riding on a donkey—even on a donkey's colt. I will remove the battle chariots from Israel and the warhorses from Jerusalem, and I will destroy all the weapons used in battle. Your king will bring peace to the nations. His realm will stretch from sea to sea and from the Euphrates River to the ends of the earth. (Zechariah 9:9–10)

Pause to offer your own expressions of thanksgiving.

Concluding Prayer

May the LORD bless you and protect you. May the LORD smile on you and be gracious to you. May the LORD show you his favor and give you his peace. (Numbers 6:24–26)

Day 4

Praise and Worship

There is no other God but me—a just God and a Savior—
no, not one! Let all the world look to me for salvation!
For I am God; there is no other. (Isaiah 45:21–22)

Pause to express your thoughts of praise and worship.

Personal Examination

My sins are piled up before God and testify against me.
Yes, I know what a sinner I am. I know that I have rebelled against the LORD. I have turned my back on God.
I know how unfair and oppressive I have been, carefully
planning my deceitful lies. (Isaiah 59:12–13)

*Ask the Spirit to search your heart and reveal any areas of
unconfessed sin. Acknowledge these to the Lord and thank
him for his forgiveness.*

Commitment

Christ has been raised from the dead. He has become
the first of a great harvest of those who will be raised
to life again. Just as death came into the world through
a man, Adam, now the resurrection from the dead has
begun through another man, Christ. Everyone dies
because all of us are related to Adam, the first man.
But all who are related to Christ, the other man, will
be given new life. But there is an order to this resurrection: Christ was raised first; then when Christ comes

back, all his people will be raised. After that the end will come, when he will turn the Kingdom over to God the Father, having put down all enemies of every kind. For Christ must reign until he humbles all his enemies beneath his feet. And the last enemy to be destroyed is death. (1 Corinthians 15:20–26)

Adam, the first man, was made from the dust of the earth, while Christ, the second man, came from heaven. Every human being has an earthly body just like Adam's, but our heavenly bodies will be just like Christ's. Just as we are now like Adam, the man of the earth, so we will someday be like Christ, the man from heaven. (1 Corinthians 15:47–49)

Pause to add your own prayers for commitment and renewal.

Personal Concerns

It is a message to obey, not just to listen to. If you don't obey, you are only fooling yourself. (James 1:22)

Spiritual Insight
Pause to ask that the Holy Spirit would give you understanding and insight into the word of truth, so that you will have a growing grasp of your identity in Christ—where you came from, who you are, and where you are going. Ask for a clearer understanding of God's purpose for your life.

Concerns for Others

God knows how often I pray for you. Day and night I bring you and your needs in prayer to God, whom

I serve with all my heart by telling others the Good News about his Son. (Romans 1:9)

Other Believers

Intercede in the lives of your personal friends, and ask that the Lord will bless their families, their careers, and their ministries. Pray that he will comfort and strengthen those who are oppressed and in need.

Prayer of Thanksgiving

Even I, the Son of Man, came here not to be served but to serve others, and to give my life as a ransom for many. (Matthew 20:28)

Jesus took a loaf of bread and asked God's blessing on it. Then he broke it in pieces and gave it to the disciples, saying, "Take it and eat it, for this is my body." And he took a cup of wine and gave thanks to God for it. He gave it to them and said, "Each of you drink from it, for this is my blood, which seals the covenant between God and his people. It is poured out to forgive the sins of many." (Matthew 26:26–28)

Pause to offer your own expressions of thanksgiving.

Concluding Prayer

Stand up and praise the LORD your God, for he lives from everlasting to everlasting! Praise his glorious name! It is far greater than we can think or say. (Nehemiah 9:5)

Day 5

Praise and Worship

LORD, through all the generations you have been our home! Before the mountains were created, before you made the earth and the world, you are God, without beginning or end. You turn people back to dust, saying, "Return to dust!" For you, a thousand years are as yesterday! They are like a few hours! (Psalm 90:1–4)

Jesus Christ is the same yesterday, today, and forever. (Hebrews 13:8)

Pause to express your thoughts of praise and worship.

Personal Examination

Then Peter came to him and asked, "Lord, how often should I forgive someone who sins against me? Seven times?" "No!" Jesus replied, "seventy times seven!" (Matthew 18:21–22)

Ask the Spirit to search your heart and reveal any areas of unconfessed sin. Acknowledge these to the Lord and thank him for his forgiveness.

Commitment

May I not worry about everyday life—whether I have enough food, drink, and clothes. Life consists of more than food and clothing. The birds don't need to plant or harvest or put food in barns because their heavenly Father feeds them. And I am far more valuable to him than they are. Can all my worries add a single moment to my life? Of course not. And why worry about my clothes? The lilies grow. They don't work or make their clothing, yet Solomon in all his glory was not dressed as beautifully as they are. And if God cares so wonderfully for flowers that are here today and gone tomorrow, won't he more surely care for me? I have so little faith! May I not worry about having enough food or drink or clothing and not be like the pagans who are so deeply concerned about these things. My heavenly Father already knows all my needs, and he will give me all I need from day to day if I live for him and make the Kingdom of God my primary concern. (Matthew 6:25–33; Luke 12:22–31)

May I not see things merely from a human point of view, but from God's. (Mark 8:33)

Pause to add your own prayers for commitment and renewal.

Personal Concerns

My heart was once full of darkness, but now I am full of light from the Lord, and my behavior should show it! For this light within me produces only what is good and right and true. May I find out what is pleasing to the Lord. (Ephesians 5:8–10)

Love and Compassion
Pause to ask for the grace of greater love and compassion for others. Pray that you will become a more Christlike person

who considers the needs of others above your own, knowing that God is your provider and sustainer.

Concerns for Others

Satan, the god of this evil world, has blinded the minds of those who don't believe, so they are unable to see the glorious light of the Good News that is shining upon them. They don't understand the message we preach about the glory of Christ, who is the exact likeness of God. (2 Corinthians 4:4)

Christian Witness

Pray on behalf of the people you personally know who have not yet entered into the joy of a personal relationship with Jesus. Intercede for your unsaved relatives, neighbors, co-workers, and friends.

Prayer of Thanksgiving

You have sorrow now, but I will see you again; then you will rejoice, and no one can rob you of that joy. At that time you won't need to ask me for anything. The truth is, you can go directly to the Father and ask him, and he will grant your request because you use my name. Ask, using my name, and you will receive, and you will have abundant joy. (John 16:22–24)

The Father himself loves me dearly because I love Jesus and believe that he came from God. (John 16:27)

Pause to offer your own expressions of thanksgiving.

Concluding Prayer

The law of the LORD is perfect, reviving the soul. The decrees of the LORD are trustworthy, making wise the simple. The commandments of the LORD are right, bringing joy to the heart. The commands of the LORD are clear, giving insight to life. Reverence for the LORD is pure, lasting forever. The laws of the LORD are true; each one is fair. They are more desirable than gold, even the finest gold. They are sweeter than honey, even honey dripping from the comb. They are a warning to those who hear them; there is great reward for those who obey them. (Psalm 19:7–11)

Day 6

Praise and Worship

How precious are your thoughts about me, O God! They are innumerable! I can't even count them; they outnumber the grains of sand! And when I wake up in the morning, you are still with me! (Psalm 139:17–18)

To whom will I compare you? Who is your equal? (Isaiah 46:5)

Pause to express your thoughts of praise and worship.

Personal Examination

O LORD, you alone can heal me; you alone can save. My praises are for you alone! (Jeremiah 17:14)

Ask the Spirit to search your heart and reveal any areas of unconfessed sin. Acknowledge these to the Lord and thank him for his forgiveness.

Commitment

And this is what he says to all humanity: "The fear of the LORD is true wisdom; to forsake evil is real understanding." (Job 28:28)

Who are those who fear the LORD? He will show them the path they should choose. (Psalm 25:12)

How happy are those who fear the LORD—all who follow his ways! (Psalm 128:1)

The LORD's delight is in those who honor him, those who put their hope in his unfailing love. (Psalm 147:11)

Pause to add your own prayers for commitment and renewal.

Personal Concerns

Whatever I do, may I do all for the glory of God. (1 Corinthians 10:31)

Faithfulness as a Steward

Pause to ask that God would empower you to become a more faithful and effective steward with all that he has entrusted to your care. Since he has given you a stewardship of talents, treasure, truth, time, and love and compassion, ask that you would use these gifts with fidelity in his service.

Concerns for Others

Show respect for everyone. Love your Christian brothers and sisters. Fear God. Show respect for the king. (1 Peter 2:17)

Government

Lift up those in local, state, and national government, and pray that those in positions of authority would look to God for wisdom in their decisions and practice.

Prayer of Thanksgiving

When we were utterly helpless, Christ came at just the right time and died for us sinners. Now, no one is likely

225

to die for a good person, though someone might be willing to die for a person who is especially good. But God showed his great love for us by sending Christ to die for us while we were still sinners. (Romans 5:6–8)

Since I have been made right in God's sight by the blood of Christ, he will certainly save me from his judgment. For since I was restored to friendship with God by the death of his Son while I was still his enemy, I will certainly be delivered from eternal punishment by his life. So now I can rejoice in our wonderful new relationship with God—all because of what my Lord Jesus Christ has done for me in making me a friend of God. (Romans 5:9–11)

Pause to offer your own expressions of thanksgiving.

Concluding Prayer

The LORD has already told me what is good, and this is what he requires of me: to do what is right, to love mercy, and to walk humbly with my God. (Micah 6:8)

Each of us will stand personally before the judgment seat of God. For the Scriptures say, "As surely as I live," says the Lord, "every knee will bow to me and every tongue will confess allegiance to God." Yes, each of us will have to give a personal account to God. (Romans 14:10b–12)

Day 7

Praise and Worship

You are the high and lofty one who inhabits eternity, and you say: "I live in that high and holy place with those whose spirits are contrite and humble. I refresh the humble and give new courage to those with repentant hearts." (Isaiah 57:15)

The procession and the crowds all around Jesus were shouting, "Praise God for the Son of David! Bless the one who comes in the name of the Lord! Praise God in highest heaven!" (Matthew 21:9)

Pause to express your thoughts of praise and worship.

Personal Examination

Who may climb the mountain of the LORD? Who may stand in his holy place? Only those whose hands and hearts are pure, who do not worship idols and never tell lies. (Psalm 24:3–4)

Ask the Spirit to search your heart and reveal any areas of unconfessed sin. Acknowledge these to the Lord and thank him for his forgiveness.

Commitment

I pray that from his glorious, unlimited resources he will give me mighty inner strength through his Holy Spirit.

I pray that Christ will be more and more at home in my heart as I trust in him. May my roots go down deep into the soil of God's marvelous love. And may I have the power to understand, as all God's people should, how wide, how long, how high, and how deep his love really is. May I experience the love of Christ, though it is so great I will never fully understand it. Then I will be filled with the fullness of life and power that comes from God. (Ephesians 3:16–19)

May I be strong with the special favor God gives me in Christ Jesus. (2 Timothy 2:1)

Pause to add your own prayers for commitment and renewal.

Personal Concerns

May I be careful and watch out! May I be very careful never to forget what I have seen you do for me. May I not let these things escape from my mind as long as I live! I will be sure to pass them on to my children and grandchildren. (Deuteronomy 4:9)

Family and Ministry

Pause to lift up your family, your career, and your ministry before the Lord. Ask that you would have the privilege of sharing Christ with others and helping people grow in their knowledge of him.

Concerns for Others

Listen to me, dear brothers and sisters. Hasn't God chosen the poor in this world to be rich in faith? Aren't they the ones who will inherit the Kingdom he promised to those who love him? (James 2:5)

Missions

Intercede for national and world missions, and pray that those who have dedicated their lives to the fulfillment of the Great Commission will be strengthened, encouraged, and empowered.

Prayer of Thanksgiving

I am not worthy of all the faithfulness and unfailing love you have shown to me, your servant. When I left home, I owned nothing except a walking stick, and now my household fills two camps! (Genesis 32:10)

You answered my prayers when I was in distress, and you have stayed with me wherever I have gone. (Genesis 35:3)

But his bow remained strong, and his arms were strengthened by the Mighty One of Jacob, the Shepherd, the Rock of Israel. (Genesis 49:24–25)

Pause to offer your own expressions of thanksgiving.

Concluding Prayer

For the LORD is a great God, the great King above all gods. The sea belongs to him, for he made it. His hands formed the dry land, too. Come, let us worship and bow down. Let us kneel before the LORD our maker, for he is our God. We are the people he watches over, the sheep under his care. Oh, that you would listen to his voice today! (Psalm 95:3–5, 7)

Shout with joy to the LORD, O earth! Worship the LORD with gladness. Come before him, singing with joy. Acknowledge that the LORD is God! He made us, and we are his. We are his people, the sheep of his pasture. (Psalm 100:1–3)

Day 8

Praise and Worship

Then David praised the LORD in the presence of the whole assembly: "O LORD, the God of our ancestor Israel, may you be praised forever and ever! Yours, O LORD, is the greatness, the power, the glory, the victory, and the majesty. Everything in the heavens and on earth is yours, O LORD, and this is your kingdom. We adore you as the one who is over all things. Riches and honor come from you alone, for you rule over everything. Power and might are in your hand, and it is at your discretion that people are made great and given strength. O our God, we thank you and praise your glorious name!" (1 Chronicles 29:10–13)

I will proclaim the name of the LORD; how glorious is our God! (Deuteronomy 32:3)

Pause to express your thoughts of praise and worship.

Personal Examination

Every time you punished us you were being just. We have sinned greatly, and you gave us only what we deserved. (Nehemiah 9:33)

Ask the Spirit to search your heart and reveal any areas of unconfessed sin. Acknowledge these to the Lord and thank him for his forgiveness.

Commitment

May I fear the LORD and sincerely worship him, thinking of all the wonderful things he has done for me. (1 Samuel 12:24)

May I not disobey the LORD's commands so that I can prosper. I will not abandon the LORD, and he will not abandon me! (2 Chronicles 24:20)

Pause to add your own prayers for commitment and renewal.

Personal Concerns

May I be respected and have integrity. May I not drink heavily or be greedy for money. I must be committed to the revealed truths of the Christian faith and must live with a clear conscience. (1 Timothy 3:8–9)

Growth in Character

Pause to look to the Lord for the power to stand firm in the spiritual warfare against the world, the flesh, and spiritual forces of wickedness. Ask that you would grow in character and pursue the disciplines of the faith in a spirit of radical dependence upon him.

Concerns for Others

LORD, be merciful to us, for we have waited for you. Be our strength each day and our salvation in times of trouble. The enemy runs at the sound of your voice. (Isaiah 33:2)

World Affairs

Lift up the needs of the poor and the hungry, the oppressed and the persecuted. Pray for those in positions of authority and ask for the blessings of peace rather than conflict.

Prayer of Thanksgiving

My heart rejoices in the LORD! Oh, how the LORD has blessed me! Now I have an answer for my enemies, as I delight in your deliverance. (1 Samuel 2:1)

You reached down from heaven and rescued me; you drew me out of deep waters. You delivered me from my powerful enemies, from those who hated me and were too strong for me. (2 Samuel 22:17–18)

Pause to offer your own expressions of thanksgiving.

Concluding Prayer

May the words of my mouth and the thoughts of my heart be pleasing to you, O LORD, my rock and my redeemer. (Psalm 19:14)

Day 9

Praise and Worship

Who else has held the oceans in his hand? Who has measured off the heavens with his fingers? Who else knows the weight of the earth or has weighed out the mountains and the hills? (Isaiah 40:12)

You are the LORD; there is no other God. You have prepared me, so all the world from east to west will know there is no other God. You are the LORD, and there is no other. (Isaiah 45:5–6)

Pause to express your thoughts of praise and worship.

Personal Examination

Thank you, LORD, that you have said: "For a brief moment I abandoned you, but with great compassion I will take you back. In a moment of anger I turned my face away for a little while. But with everlasting love I will have compassion on you." (Isaiah 54:7–8)

Ask the Spirit to search your heart and reveal any areas of unconfessed sin. Acknowledge these to the Lord and thank him for his forgiveness.

Commitment

Christ came once for all time, at the end of the age, to remove the power of sin forever by his sacrificial death for us. And just as it is destined that each person dies only once and after that comes judgment, so also Christ died only once as a sacrifice to take away the sins of many people. He will come again but not to deal with our sins again. This time he will bring salvation to all those who are eagerly waiting for him. (Hebrews 9:26–28)

God chose Jesus long before the world began, but now in these final days, he has been sent to the earth for all to see. And he did this for me. Through Christ I have come to trust in God. And because God raised Christ from the dead and gave him great glory, may I place my faith and hope confidently in God. (1 Peter 1:20–21)

Pause to add your own prayers for commitment and renewal.

Personal Concerns

May your unfailing love comfort me, just as you promised me, your servant. (Psalm 119:76)

Knowing, Loving, and Trusting God
Pause to ask God for the grace to know and please him. Ask him to enlarge your capacity to love him more and abide wholly in him.

Concerns for Others

How wonderful it is, how pleasant, when brothers live together in harmony! (Psalm 133:1)

Churches and Ministries

Ask God to work on behalf of the people and concerns at your local church. Pray for his blessing and power in the ministries that are engaged in Christian witness, discipleship, education, and those serving people in need.

Prayer of Thanksgiving

I cried out to the LORD in my suffering, and he heard me. He set me free from all my fears. For the angel of the LORD guards all who fear him, and he rescues them. (Psalm 34:6–7)

I waited patiently for the LORD to help me, and he turned to me and heard my cry. He lifted me out of the pit of despair, out of the mud and the mire. He set my feet on solid ground and steadied me as I walked along. He has given me a new song to sing, a hymn of praise to our God. Many will see what he has done and be astounded. They will put their trust in the LORD. (Psalm 40:1–3)

Pause to offer your own expressions of thanksgiving.

Concluding Prayer

The LORD is my rock, my fortress, and my savior; my God is my rock, in whom I find protection. He is my shield, the strength of my salvation, and my stronghold, my high tower, my savior, the one who saves me from violence. I will call on the LORD, who is worthy of praise, for he saves me from my enemies. (2 Samuel 22:2–4)

Day 10

Praise and Worship

You are dressed in a robe of light. You stretch out the starry curtain of the heavens; you lay out the rafters of your home in the rain clouds. You make the clouds your chariots; you ride upon the wings of the wind. The winds are your messengers; flames of fire are your servants. You placed the world on its foundation so it would never be moved. You clothed the earth with floods of water, water that covered even the mountains. At the sound of your rebuke, the water fled; at the sound of your thunder, it fled away. Mountains rose and valleys sank to the levels you decreed. Then you set a firm boundary for the seas, so they would never again cover the earth. O LORD, what a variety of things you have made! In wisdom you have made them all. The earth is full of your creatures. (Psalm 104:2–9, 24)

Pause to express your thoughts of praise and worship.

Personal Examination

When I had lost all hope, I turned my thoughts once more to the LORD. And my earnest prayer went out to you in your holy Temple. Those who worship false gods turn their backs on all God's mercies. But I will offer sacrifices to you with songs of praise, and I will fulfill all my vows. For my salvation comes from the LORD alone. (Jonah 2:7–9)

Ask the Spirit to search your heart and reveal any areas of unconfessed sin. Acknowledge these to the Lord and thank him for his forgiveness.

Commitment

As a servant of Christ who has been put in charge of explaining God's secrets, and as a manager of his possessions, I must be faithful. (1 Corinthians 4:1–2)

People who long to be rich fall into temptation and are trapped by many foolish and harmful desires that plunge them into ruin and destruction. For the love of money is at the root of all kinds of evil. And some people, craving money, have wandered from the faith and pierced themselves with many sorrows. But may I belong to God; and so run from all these evil things, and follow what is right and good. May I pursue a godly life, along with faith, love, perseverance, and gentleness. (1 Timothy 6:9–11)

Pause to add your own prayers for commitment and renewal.

Personal Concerns

Joseph said to his brothers: "Don't be angry with yourselves that you did this to me, for God did it. He sent me here ahead of you to preserve your lives. These two years of famine will grow to seven, during which there will be neither plowing nor harvest. God has sent me here to keep you and your families alive so that you will become a great nation. Yes, it was God who sent me here, not you! And he has made me a counselor to

Pharaoh—manager of his entire household and ruler over all Egypt." (Genesis 45:5, 7–8)

Like Joseph, may I seek your perspective on the circumstances of my life.

Greater Wisdom

Pause to ask God for the grace to develop an eternal perspective on your life and concerns, and that he would renew your mind with his truth. Ask for the power to order your steps with wisdom and skill in each area of life so that you will seek to please him rather than impress others.

Concerns for Others

Be humble and gentle. Be patient with each other, making allowance for each other's faults because of your love. Always keep yourselves united in the Holy Spirit, and bind yourselves together with peace. (Ephesians 4:2–3)

Loved Ones

Lift up the members of your immediate family and your extended family. Pray for the spiritual, emotional, and physical concerns of your loved ones.

Prayer of Thanksgiving

The creation of the heavens and the earth and everything in them was completed. On the seventh day, having finished his task, God rested from all his work. (Genesis 2:1–2)

LORD God, You formed man from the dust of the ground and breathed life into him. (Genesis 2:10)

Pause to offer your own expressions of thanksgiving.

Concluding Prayer

And I am convinced that nothing can ever separate us from his love. Death can't, and life can't. The angels can't, and the demons can't. Our fears for today, our worries about tomorrow, and even the powers of hell can't keep God's love away. Whether we are high above the sky or in the deepest ocean, nothing in all creation will ever be able to separate us from the love of God that is revealed in Christ Jesus our Lord. (Romans 8:38–39)

Day 11

Praise and Worship

As the deer pants for streams of water, so I long for you, O God. I thirst for God, the living God. When can I come and stand before him? (Psalm 42:1–2)

All night long I search for you; earnestly I seek for God. For only when you come to judge the earth will people turn from wickedness and do what is right. (Isaiah 26:9)

Pause to express your thoughts of praise and worship.

Personal Examination

I will not forget the encouraging words God spoke to me, his child. He said, "My child, don't ignore it when the Lord disciplines you, and don't be discouraged when he corrects you. For the Lord disciplines those he loves, and he punishes those he accepts as his children." (Hebrews 12:5–6)

Ask the Spirit to search your heart and reveal any areas of unconfessed sin. Acknowledge these to the Lord and thank him for his forgiveness.

Commitment

Many who seem to be important now will be the least important then, and those who are considered least here will be the greatest then. (Matthew 19:30; Mark 10:31)

Whoever wants to be a leader among you must be your servant, and whoever wants to be first must be the slave of all. For even you, Son of Man, came here not to be served but to serve others, and to give your life as a ransom for many. (Matthew 20:26–27; Mark 10:43–44)

Those who exalt themselves will be humbled, and those who humble themselves will be exalted. (Matthew 23:12; Luke 14:11; 18:14)

Pause to add your own prayers for commitment and renewal.

Personal Concerns

May I be one whose life cannot be spoken against. May I be faithful and self-controlled, live wisely and have a good reputation, enjoy having guests in my home, and be able to teach. May I not drink heavily or be violent. I must be gentle, peace loving, and not one who loves money. I must manage my own family well, with children who respect and obey me. Grant me respect among the people outside the church so that I will not fall into the Devil's trap and be disgraced. (1 Timothy 3:2–4, 7)

Spiritual Insight

Pause to ask that the Holy Spirit would give you understanding and insight into the word of truth, so that you will have a growing grasp of your identity in Christ—where you came from, who you are, and where you are going. Ask for a clearer understanding of God's purpose for your life.

Concerns for Others

The Holy Spirit helps us in our distress. For we don't even know what we should pray for, nor how we should pray. But the Holy Spirit prays for us with groanings that cannot be expressed in words. And the Father who knows all hearts knows what the Spirit is saying, for the Spirit pleads for us believers in harmony with God's own will. (Romans 8:26–27)

Other Believers

Intercede in the lives of your personal friends, and ask that the Lord will bless their families, their careers, and their ministries. Pray that he will comfort and strengthen those who are oppressed and in need.

Prayer of Thanksgiving

God saved me by his special favor when I believed. And I can't take credit for this; it is a gift from God. Salvation is not a reward for the good things I have done, so none of us can boast about it. (Ephesians 2:8–9)

And I am sure that God, who began the good work within me, will continue his work until it is finally finished on that day when Christ Jesus comes back again. (Philippians 1:6)

Pause to offer your own expressions of thanksgiving.

Concluding Prayer

God raised Jesus up to the heights of heaven and gave him a name that is above every other name, so that at the name of Jesus every knee will bow, in heaven and on earth and under the earth, and every tongue will confess that Jesus Christ is Lord, to the glory of God the Father. (Philippians 2:9–11)

Christ is the head of the church, which is his body. He is the first of all who will rise from the dead, so he is first in everything. (Colossians 1:18)

Day 12

Praise and Worship

Not to us, O LORD, but to you goes all the glory for your unfailing love and faithfulness. (Psalm 115:1)

Praise the LORD! How good it is to sing praises to our God! How delightful and how right! (Psalm 147:1)

Pause to express your thoughts of praise and worship.

Personal Examination

Who among you fears the LORD and obeys his servant? If you are walking in darkness, without a ray of light, trust in the LORD and rely on your God. (Isaiah 50:10)

Ask the Spirit to search your heart and reveal any areas of unconfessed sin. Acknowledge these to the Lord and thank him for his forgiveness.

Commitment

May I be a faithful person who fears God. (Nehemiah 7:2)

I have hope in God, just as these men do, that he will raise both the righteous and the ungodly. Because of this, I always try to maintain a clear conscience before God and everyone else. (Acts 24:15–16)

Pause to add your own prayers for commitment and renewal.

Personal Concerns

Listen closely to my prayer, O LORD; hear my urgent cry. I will call to you whenever trouble strikes, and you will answer me. For you are great and perform great miracles. You alone are God. (Psalm 86:6–7, 10)

Love and Compassion

Pause to ask for the grace of greater love and compassion for others. Pray that you will become a more Christlike person who considers the needs of others above your own, knowing that God is your provider and sustainer.

Concerns for Others

Grant that I may be used to open people's eyes so they may turn from darkness to light, and from the power of Satan to God. Then they will receive forgiveness for their sins and be given a place among God's people, who are set apart by faith in you. (Acts 26:18)

Christian Witness

Pray on behalf of the people you personally know who have not yet entered into the joy of a personal relationship with Jesus. Intercede for your unsaved relatives, neighbors, co-workers, and friends.

Prayer of Thanksgiving

In the beginning you created the heavens and the earth. The earth was empty, a formless mass cloaked in darkness. And your Spirit was hovering over its surface. Then you said, "Let there be light," and there was light. And you saw that it was good. Then you separated the light from the darkness. You called the light "day" and the darkness "night." Together these made up one day. And you said, "Let there be space between the waters, to separate water from water." And so it was. You made this space to separate the waters above from the waters below. And you called the space "sky." This happened on the second day. And you said, "Let the waters beneath the sky be gathered into one place so dry ground may appear." And so it was. You named the dry ground "land" and the water "seas." And you saw that it was good. (Genesis 1:1–10)

Pause to offer your own expressions of thanksgiving.

Concluding Prayer

My life passes as swiftly as the evening shadows. I am withering like grass. But you, O LORD, will rule forever. Your fame will endure to every generation. In ages past you laid the foundation of the earth, and the heavens are the work of your hands. Even they will perish, but you remain forever; they will wear out like old clothing. You will change them like a garment, and they will fade away. But you are always the same; your years never end. My days are like a lengthened shadow. (Psalm 102:11–12, 25–27)

Day 13

Praise and Worship

The LORD, the LORD Almighty, touches the land and it melts, and all its people mourn. The ground rises like the Nile River at flood time, and then it sinks again. The upper stories of the LORD's home are in the heavens, while its foundation is on the earth. He draws up water from the oceans and pours it down as rain on the land. The LORD is his name! (Amos 9:5–6)

Pause to express your thoughts of praise and worship.

Personal Examination

Why should we, mere humans, complain when we are punished for our sins? Instead, let us test and examine our ways. Let us turn again in repentance to the LORD. (Lamentations 3:39–40)

Ask the Spirit to search your heart and reveal any areas of unconfessed sin. Acknowledge these to the Lord and thank him for his forgiveness.

Commitment

May I not copy the behavior and customs of this world, but let God transform me into a new person by changing the way I think. Then I will know what God wants me to do, and I will know how good and pleasing and perfect his will really is. (Romans 12:2)

May God, the glorious Father of our Lord Jesus Christ, give me spiritual wisdom and understanding, so that I might grow in my knowledge of God. I pray that my heart will be flooded with light so that I can understand the wonderful future he has promised to me. I want to realize what a rich and glorious inheritance he has given to me. I pray that I will begin to understand the incredible greatness of his power for me, because I believe. (Ephesians 1:17–19)

Pause to add your own prayers for commitment and renewal.

Personal Concerns

May I not be influenced by bad examples but follow only what is good. I will remember that those who do good prove that they are God's children, and those who do evil prove that they do not know God. (3 John 11)

Faithfulness as a Steward
Pause to ask that God would empower you to become a more faithful and effective steward with all that he has entrusted to your care. Since he has given you a stewardship of talents, treasure, truth, time, and love and compassion, ask that you would use these gifts with fidelity in his service.

Concerns for Others

Remind your people to submit to the government and its officers. They should be obedient, always ready to do what is good. They must not speak evil of anyone, and they must avoid quarreling. Instead, they should be gentle and show true humility to everyone. (Titus 3:1–2)

249

Government

Lift up those in local, state, and national government, and pray that those in positions of authority would look to God for wisdom in their decisions and practice.

Prayer of Thanksgiving

You faithfully answer our prayers with awesome deeds, O God our savior. You are the hope of everyone on earth, even those who sail on distant seas. You formed the mountains by your power and armed yourself with mighty strength. You quieted the raging oceans with their pounding waves and silenced the shouting of the nations. (Psalm 65:5–7)

Pause to offer your own expressions of thanksgiving.

Concluding Prayer

When I saw him, I fell at his feet as dead. But he laid his right hand on me and said, "Don't be afraid! I am the First and the Last. I am the living one who died. Look, I am alive forever and ever! And I hold the keys of death and the grave." (Revelation 1:17–18)

The Lamb is worthy—the Lamb who was killed. He is worthy to receive power and riches and wisdom and strength and honor and glory and blessing. (Revelation 5:12)

Day 14

Praise and Worship

All he does is just and good, and all his commandments are trustworthy. They are forever true, to be obeyed faithfully and with integrity. He has paid a full ransom for his people. He has guaranteed his covenant with them forever. What a holy, awe-inspiring name he has! (Psalm 111:7–9)

Your name, O Lord, endures forever; your fame, O Lord, is known to every generation. (Psalm 135:13)

Pause to express your thoughts of praise and worship.

Personal Examination

I know, Lord, that a person's life is not his own. No one is able to plan his own course. So correct me, Lord, but please be gentle. Do not correct me in anger, for I would die. (Jeremiah 10:23–24)

Ask the Spirit to search your heart and reveal any areas of unconfessed sin. Acknowledge these to the Lord and thank him for his forgiveness.

Commitment

Like Noah, may I be a righteous and blameless man who consistently follows God's will and enjoys a close relationship with him. (Genesis 6:9)

Like Moses, may I do according to all the LORD's instructions. (Exodus 39:42; 40:16)

Pause to add your own prayers for commitment and renewal.

Personal Concerns

I pray that all is well with you and that your body is as healthy as I know your soul is. (3 John 2)

Family and Ministry

Pause to lift up your family, your career, and your ministry before the Lord. Ask that you would have the privilege of sharing Christ with others and helping people grow in their knowledge of him.

Concerns for Others

Remember this good deed, O my God, and do not forget all that I have faithfully done for the Temple of my God. (Nehemiah 13:14, 31)

Missions

Intercede for national and world missions, and pray that those who have dedicated their lives to the fulfillment of the Great Commission will be strengthened, encouraged, and empowered.

Prayer of Thanksgiving

I saw the holy city, the new Jerusalem, coming down from God out of heaven like a beautiful bride prepared for her husband. I heard a loud shout from the throne, saying, "Look, the home of God is now among his people! He will live with them, and they will be his people. God himself will be with them. He will remove all of their sorrows, and there will be no more death or sorrow or crying or pain. For the old world and its evils are gone forever." And the one sitting on the throne said, "Look, I am making all things new!" (Revelation 21:2–5)

Pause to offer your own expressions of thanksgiving.

Concluding Prayer

The LORD, your Redeemer, the Holy One of Israel, says: I am the LORD your God, who teaches you what is good and leads you along the paths you should follow. (Isaiah 48:17)

Jesus, you have said, "Come to me, all of you who are weary and carry heavy burdens, and I will give you rest. Take my yoke upon you. Let me teach you, because I am humble and gentle, and you will find rest for your souls. For my yoke fits perfectly, and the burden I give you is light." (Matthew 11:28–30)

Day 15

Praise and Worship

The Most High rules over the kingdoms of the world and gives them to anyone he chooses—even to the lowliest of humans. I will praise and worship the Most High and honor the one who lives forever. His rule is everlasting, and his kingdom is eternal. All the people of the earth are nothing compared to him. He has the power to do as he pleases among the angels of heaven and with those who live on earth. No one can stop him or challenge him, saying, "What do you mean by doing these things?" (Daniel 4:17, 34–35, 37)

I will bless the Most High. I praise and glorify and honor the King of heaven. All his acts are just and true, and he is able to humble those who are proud. (Daniel 4:17, 34–35, 37)

Pause to express your thoughts of praise and worship.

Personal Examination

You will cleanse away my sins and will forgive all the sins of my rebellion. (Jeremiah 33:8)

Ask the Spirit to search your heart and reveal any areas of unconfessed sin. Acknowledge these to the Lord and thank him for his forgiveness.

Commitment

May I make every effort to apply the benefits of his promises to my life. Then my faith will produce a life of moral excellence. A life of moral excellence leads to knowing God better. Knowing God leads to self-control. Self-control leads to patient endurance, and patient endurance leads to godliness. Godliness leads to love for other Christians, and finally I will grow to have genuine love for everyone. The more I grow like this, the more I will become productive and useful in my knowledge of my Lord Jesus Christ. (2 Peter 1:5–8)

Pause to add your own prayers for commitment and renewal.

Personal Concerns

Hear my prayer, O LORD; listen to my plea! Answer me because you are faithful and righteous. (Psalm 143:1)

Growth in Character

Pause to look to the Lord for the power to stand firm in the spiritual warfare against the world, the flesh, and spiritual forces of wickedness. Ask that you would grow in character and pursue the disciplines of the faith in a spirit of radical dependence upon him.

Concerns for Others

I know the LORD will surely help those they persecute; he will maintain the rights of the poor. (Psalm 140:12)

World Affairs

Lift up the needs of the poor and the hungry, the oppressed and the persecuted. Pray for those in positions of authority and ask for the blessings of peace rather than conflict.

Prayer of Thanksgiving

Because God's children are human beings—made of flesh and blood—Jesus also became flesh and blood by being born in human form. For only as a human being could he die, and only by dying could he break the power of the Devil, who had the power of death. Only in this way could he deliver those who have lived all their lives as slaves to the fear of dying. (Hebrews 2:14–15)

It was necessary for Jesus to be in every respect like us, his brothers and sisters, so that he could be our merciful and faithful High Priest before God. He then could offer a sacrifice that would take away the sins of the people. Since he himself has gone through suffering and temptation, he is able to help us when we are being tempted. (Hebrews 2:17–18)

Pause to offer your own expressions of thanksgiving.

Concluding Prayer

Yes, the Sovereign LORD is coming in all his glorious power. He will rule with awesome strength. See, he brings his reward with him as he comes. He will feed his flock like a shepherd. He will carry the lambs in his arms, holding them close to his heart. He will gently lead the mother sheep with their young. (Isaiah 40:10–11)

Day 16

Praise and Worship

Do not fear anything except the LORD Almighty. He alone is the Holy One. If you fear him, you need fear nothing else. (Isaiah 8:13)

He will be our sure foundation, providing a rich store of salvation, wisdom, and knowledge. The fear of the LORD is the key to this treasure. (Isaiah 33:6)

Pause to express your thoughts of praise and worship.

Personal Examination

I will sing to the LORD, all you godly ones! I will praise his holy name. His anger lasts for a moment, but his favor lasts a lifetime! Weeping may go on all night, but joy comes with the morning. (Psalm 30:4–5)

Ask the Spirit to search your heart and reveal any areas of unconfessed sin. Acknowledge these to the Lord and thank him for his forgiveness.

Commitment

May I fight the good fight for what I believe and hold tightly to the eternal life that God has given me, which I have confessed so well before many witnesses. Before God, who gives life to all, and before Christ Jesus, who gave a good testimony before Pontius Pilate, may

I obey your commands with all purity. Then no one can find fault with me from now until you return. For at the right time you will be revealed from heaven by the blessed and only almighty God. (1 Timothy 6:12–15a)

May I work hard so God can approve me; and may I be a good worker, one who does not need to be ashamed and who correctly explains the word of truth. (2 Timothy 2:15)

Pause to add your own prayers for commitment and renewal.

Personal Concerns

Do not use dishonest standards when measuring length, weight, or volume. Your scales and weights must be accurate. Your containers for measuring dry goods or liquids must be accurate. I, the LORD, am your God, who brought you out of the land of Egypt. (Leviticus 19:35–36)

Knowing, Loving, and Trusting God
Pause to ask God for the grace to know and please him. Ask him to enlarge your capacity to love him more and abide wholly in him.

Concerns for Others

The kind of fasting you want calls me to free those who are wrongly imprisoned and to stop oppressing those who work for me, to treat them fairly and give them what they earn. You want me to share my food with the hungry and to welcome poor wanderers into my home, to give clothes to those who need them, and not hide from relatives who need my help. If I do these things, my salvation will come like the dawn. Yes, my healing will come quickly. My godliness will lead me forward, and the glory of the LORD will protect me from behind. Then when I call, the LORD will answer. "Yes, I am here," he will quickly reply. If we stop oppressing the helpless and stop making false accusations and spreading vicious rumors and feed the hungry and help those in trouble, then our light will shine out from the darkness, and the darkness around us will be as bright as day. (Isaiah 58:6–10)

Churches and Ministries

Ask God to work on behalf of the people and concerns at your local church. Pray for his blessing and power in the ministries that are engaged in Christian witness, discipleship, education, and those serving people in need.

Prayer of Thanksgiving

God will keep me strong right up to the end, and he will keep me free from all blame on the great day when our Lord Jesus Christ returns. God will surely do this for me, for he always does just what he says, and he is the one who invited me into this wonderful friendship with his Son, Jesus Christ our Lord. (1 Corinthians 1:8–9)

No eye has seen, no ear has heard, and no mind has imagined what God has prepared for those who love him. (1 Corinthians 2:9)

Pause to offer your own expressions of thanksgiving.

Concluding Prayer

You are worthy, O Lord our God, to receive glory and honor and power. For you created everything, and it is for your pleasure that they exist and were created. (Revelation 4:11)

Blessing and honor and glory and power belong to the one sitting on the throne and to the Lamb forever and ever. (Revelation 5:13)

Day 17

Praise and Worship

"My thoughts are completely different from yours," says the Lord. "And my ways are far beyond anything you could imagine. For just as the heavens are higher than the earth, so are my ways higher than your ways and my thoughts higher than your thoughts." (Isaiah 55:8–9)

You are the Lord, the God of all the peoples of the world. Is anything is too hard for you? (Jeremiah 32:27)

Pause to express your thoughts of praise and worship.

Personal Examination

O Lord, God of heaven, the great and awesome God who keeps his covenant of unfailing love with those who love him and obey his commands, listen to my prayer! Look down and see me praying night and day for your people. I confess that we have sinned against you. Yes, even my own family and I have sinned! (Nehemiah 1:5–6)

Ask the Spirit to search your heart and reveal any areas of unconfessed sin. Acknowledge these to the Lord and thank him for his forgiveness.

Commitment

You must obey all my regulations and be careful to keep my laws, for I, the LORD, am your God. If you obey my laws and regulations, you will find life through them. I am the LORD. (Leviticus 18:4–5)

Pause to add your own prayers for commitment and renewal.

Personal Concerns

You have died with Christ, and he has set you free from the evil powers of this world. May I not keep on following rules of the world. (Colossians 2:20)

Greater Wisdom

Pause to ask God for the grace to develop an eternal perspective on your life and concerns, and that he would renew your mind with his truth. Ask for the power to order your steps with wisdom and skill in each area of life so that you will seek to please him rather than impress others.

Concerns for Others

I must commit myself wholeheartedly to the commands you give me. I will repeat them again and again to my children. I will talk about them when I am at home and when I am away on a journey, when I am lying down and when I am getting up again. (Deuteronomy 6:6–7)

Loved Ones

Lift up the members of your immediate family and your extended family. Pray for the spiritual, emotional, and physical concerns of your loved ones.

Prayer of Thanksgiving

Surely the godly are praising your name, for they will live in your presence. (Psalm 140:13)

The Lord is close to all who call on him, yes, to all who call on him sincerely. He fulfills the desires of those who fear him; he hears their cries for help and rescues them. The Lord protects all those who love him, but he destroys the wicked. (Psalm 145:18–20)

Pause to offer your own expressions of thanksgiving.

Concluding Prayer

The Lord said, "I will make all my goodness pass before you, and I will call out my name, 'the Lord,' to you. I will show kindness to anyone I choose, and I will show mercy to anyone I choose." (Exodus 33:19)

You are the Lord, the merciful and gracious God. You are slow to anger and rich in unfailing love and faithfulness. (Exodus 34:6–7)

Day 18

Praise and Worship

I watched as thrones were put in place and the Ancient One sat down to judge. His clothing was as white as snow, his hair like whitest wool. He sat on a fiery throne with wheels of blazing fire, and a river of fire flowed from his presence. Millions of angels ministered to him, and a hundred million stood to attend him. Then the court began its session, and the books were opened. (Daniel 7:9–10)

O LORD, God of Israel, you are enthroned between the mighty cherubim! You alone are God of all the kingdoms of the earth. You alone created the heavens and the earth. (2 Kings 19:15)

Pause to express your thoughts of praise and worship.

Personal Examination

Remember, O LORD, your unfailing love and compassion, which you have shown from long ages past. Forgive the rebellious sins of my youth; look instead through the eyes of your unfailing love, for you are merciful, O LORD. (Psalm 25:6–7)

Ask the Spirit to search your heart and reveal any areas of unconfessed sin. Acknowledge these to the Lord and thank him for his forgiveness.

Commitment

May I know the God of my ancestors, worship and serve him with my whole heart and with a willing mind. For the LORD sees every heart and understands and knows every plan and thought. If I seek him, I will find him. But if I forsake him, he will reject me forever. (1 Chronicles 28:9)

May I follow God's example in everything I do, because I am his dear child. May I live a life filled with love for others, following the example of Christ, who loved me and gave himself as a sacrifice to take away my sins. And God was pleased, because that sacrifice was like sweet perfume to him. (Ephesians 5:1–2)

Pause to add your own prayers for commitment and renewal.

Personal Concerns

Arise, O LORD, and let your enemies be scattered! Let them flee before you! (Numbers 10:35)

Spiritual Insight
Pause to ask that the Holy Spirit would give you under-standing and insight into the word of truth, so that you will have a growing grasp of your identity in Christ—where you came from, who you are, and where you are going. Ask for a clearer understanding of God's purpose for your life.

Concerns for Others

The Lord Jesus prayed these words for the unity of all who would believe in Him: "I pray that they will be one, just as you and I are one, Father—that just as you are in me and I am in you, so they will be in us, and the world will believe you sent me. I have given them the glory you gave me, so that they may be one, as we are— I in them and you in me, all being perfected into one. Then the world will know that you sent me and will understand that you love them as much as you love me." (John 17:21–23)

Other Believers

Intercede in the lives of your personal friends, and ask that the Lord will bless their families, their careers, and their ministries. Pray that he will comfort and strengthen those who are oppressed and in need.

Prayer of Thanksgiving

You will rescue those who love you. You will protect those who trust in your name. When I call on you, you will answer; you will be with me in trouble. You will rescue me and honor me. You will satisfy me with a long life and give me your salvation. (Psalm 91:14–16)

Pause to offer your own expressions of thanksgiving.

Concluding Prayer

As for God, his way is perfect. All the LORD's promises prove true. He is a shield for all who look to him for protection. For who is God except the LORD? Who but our God is a solid rock? (2 Samuel 22:31–32)

Day 19

Praise and Worship

The LORD is the one who shaped the mountains, stirs up the winds, and reveals his every thought. He turns the light of dawn into darkness and treads the mountains under his feet. The LORD God Almighty is his name! (Amos 4:13)

In your majesty, you dwell in the likeness of a throne of blue sapphire above the crystal surface over the heads of the cherubim. (Ezekiel 10:1)

Pause to express your thoughts of praise and worship.

Personal Examination

I am lying if I say I have fellowship with God but go on living in spiritual darkness. I am not living in the truth. But if I am living in the light of God's presence, just as Christ is, then I have fellowship with others, and the blood of Jesus, his Son, cleanses me from every sin. (1 John 1:6–7)

Ask the Spirit to search your heart and reveal any areas of unconfessed sin. Acknowledge these to the Lord and thank him for his forgiveness.

Commitment

You are God Almighty; may I serve you faithfully and live a blameless life. (Genesis 17:1)

May I love my enemies, doing good to them, lending to them! May I not be concerned that they might not repay. Then my reward from heaven will be very great, and I will truly be acting as a child of the Most High, for he is kind to the unthankful and to those who are wicked. I must be compassionate, just as my Father is compassionate. (Luke 6:35–36)

Pause to add your own prayers for commitment and renewal.

Personal Concerns

Be strong and courageous! Don't be afraid, for there is a power far greater on our side! We have the Lord our God to help us and to fight our battles for us! (2 Chronicles 32:7–8)

Love and Compassion

Pause to ask for the grace of greater love and compassion for others. Pray that you will become a more Christlike person who considers the needs of others above your own, knowing that God is your provider and sustainer.

Concerns for Others

Knowing the fear of the Lord, may I work hard to persuade men. (2 Corinthians 5:11)

Christian Witness

Pray on behalf of the people you personally know who have not yet entered into the joy of a personal relationship with Jesus. Intercede for your unsaved relatives, neighbors, co-workers, and friends.

Prayer of Thanksgiving

God has come to save me. I will trust in him and not be afraid. The LORD God is my strength and my song; he has become my salvation. (Isaiah 12:2)

I will trust in the LORD always, for the LORD God is the eternal Rock. (Isaiah 26:4)

Pause to offer your own expressions of thanksgiving.

Concluding Prayer

God is my strong fortress; he has made my way safe. He makes me as surefooted as a deer, leading me safely along the mountain heights. He prepares me for battle; he strengthens me to draw a bow of bronze. You have given me the shield of your salvation; your help has made me great. You have made a wide path for my feet to keep them from slipping. (2 Samuel 22:33–37; Psalm 18:33–36)

The LORD lives! Blessed be my Rock!
May God, the rock of my salvation, be exalted! (2 Samuel 22:47; Psalm 18:46)

Day 20

Praise and Worship

How we praise God, the Father of our Lord Jesus Christ, who has blessed us with every spiritual blessing in the heavenly realms because we belong to Christ. (Ephesians 1:3)

Our Lord Jesus Christ died for our sins, just as God our Father planned, in order to rescue us from this evil world in which we live. That is why all glory belongs to God through all the ages of eternity. Amen. (Galatians 1:3–5)

Pause to express your thoughts of praise and worship.

Personal Examination

O God, you know how foolish I am; my sins cannot be hidden from you. Don't let those who trust in you stumble because of me, O Sovereign LORD Almighty. Don't let me cause them to be humiliated, O God of Israel. (Psalm 69:5–6)

Ask the Spirit to search your heart and reveal any areas of unconfessed sin. Acknowledge these to the Lord and thank him for his forgiveness.

Commitment

Love is patient and kind. Love is not jealous or boastful or proud or rude. Love does not demand its own way. Love is not irritable, and it keeps no record of when it has been wronged. It is never glad about injustice but rejoices whenever the truth wins out. Love never gives up, never loses faith, is always hopeful, and endures through every circumstance. Love will last forever, but prophecy and speaking in unknown languages and special knowledge will all disappear. (1 Corinthians 13:4–8)

May my love for others overflow more and more, and may I keep on growing in my knowledge and under-standing. For I want to understand what really matters, so that I may live a pure and blameless life until Christ returns. May I always be filled with the fruit of my salvation—those good things that are produced in my life by Jesus Christ—for this will bring much glory and praise to God. (Philippians 1:9–11)

Pause to add your own prayers for commitment and renewal.

Personal Concerns

Listen to my pleading, O LORD. Be merciful and answer me! My heart has heard you say, "Come and talk with me." And my heart responds, "LORD, I am coming." (Psalm 27:7–8)

Faithfulness as a Steward

Pause to ask that God would empower you to become a more faithful and effective steward with all that he has entrusted to your care. Since he has given you a stewardship of talents, treasure, truth, time, and love and compassion, ask that you would use these gifts with fidelity in his service.

Concerns for Others

May I obey the government, for God is the one who put it there. All governments have been placed in power by God. So those who refuse to obey the laws of the land are refusing to obey God, and punishment will follow. (Romans 13:1–2)

Government

Lift up those in local, state, and national government, and pray that those in positions of authority would look to God for wisdom in their decisions and practice.

Prayer of Thanksgiving

Give thanks to the LORD, for he is good! His faithful love endures forever. (Psalm 118:1)

Forever, O LORD, your word stands firm in heaven. Your faithfulness extends to every generation, as enduring as the earth you created. Your laws remain true today, for everything serves your plans. (Psalm 119:89–91)

Pause to offer your own expressions of thanksgiving.

Concluding Prayer

I am confident that I will see the Lord's goodness while I am here in the land of the living. Wait patiently for the Lord. Be brave and courageous. Yes, wait patiently for the Lord. (Psalm 27:13–14)

We depend on the Lord alone to save us. Only he can help us, protecting us like a shield. In him our hearts rejoice, for we are trusting in his holy name. Let your unfailing love surround us, Lord, for our hope is in you alone. (Psalm 33:20–22)

Day 21

Praise and Worship

I will praise the LORD at all times. I will constantly speak his praises. I will boast only in the LORD; let all who are discouraged take heart. Come, let us tell of the LORD's greatness; let us exalt his name together. (Psalm 34:1–3)

The LORD is my fortress; my God is a mighty rock where I can hide. (Psalm 94:22)

Pause to express your thoughts of praise and worship.

Personal Examination

Can a mortal be just and upright before God? Can a person be pure before the Creator? (Job 4:17)

Ask the Spirit to search your heart and reveal any areas of unconfessed sin. Acknowledge these to the Lord and thank him for his forgiveness.

Commitment

May I honor my father and my mother. (Exodus 20:12; Deuteronomy 5:16)

May I not murder. (Exodus 20:13; Deuteronomy 5:17)

May I not commit adultery. (Exodus 20:14; Deuteronomy 5:18)

Pause to add your own prayers for commitment and renewal.

Personal Concerns

O Lᴏʀᴅ, do not stay away! You are my strength; come quickly to my aid! (Psalm 22:19)

Family and Ministry

Pause to lift up your family, your career, and your ministry before the Lord. Ask that you would have the privilege of sharing Christ with others and helping people grow in their knowledge of him.

Concerns for Others

Pray at all times and on every occasion in the power of the Holy Spirit. Stay alert and be persistent in your prayers for all Christians everywhere. (Ephesians 6:18)

Missions

Intercede for national and world missions, and pray that those who have dedicated their lives to the fulfillment of the Great Commission will be strengthened, encouraged, and empowered.

Prayer of Thanksgiving

You will be my God throughout my lifetime—until my hair is white with age. You made me, and you will care for me. You will carry me along and save me. (Isaiah 46:4)

As for me, I look to the LORD for his help. I wait confidently for God to save me, and my God will certainly hear me. (Micah 7:7)

Pause to offer your own expressions of thanksgiving.

Concluding Prayer

I wait quietly before God, for my salvation comes from him. He alone is my rock and my salvation, my fortress where I will never be shaken. (Psalm 62:1–2)

Blessed be the LORD, the God of Israel, from everlasting to everlasting! Let all the people say, "Amen!" Praise the LORD! (Psalm 106:48)

Day 22

Praise and Worship

Like the shout of a huge crowd, or the roar of mighty ocean waves, or the crash of loud thunder, I heard: "Hallelujah! For the Lord our God, the Almighty, reigns. Let us be glad and rejoice and honor him. For the time has come for the wedding feast of the Lamb, and his bride has prepared herself." And the angel said, "Write this: Blessed are those who are invited to the wedding feast of the Lamb." (Revelation 19:6–7, 9)

You are both the source of David and the heir to his throne. You are the bright morning star. (Revelation 22:16)

Pause to express your thoughts of praise and worship.

Personal Examination

So you should realize that just as a parent disciplines a child, the LORD your God disciplines you to help you. (Deuteronomy 8:5)

Ask the Spirit to search your heart and reveal any areas of unconfessed sin. Acknowledge these to the Lord and thank him for his forgiveness.

Commitment

May I not steal. (Exodus 20:15; Deuteronomy 5:19)

May I not testify falsely against my neighbor. (Exodus 20:16; Deuteronomy 5:20)

May I not covet my neighbor's house, and may I not covet anything else my neighbor owns. (Exodus 20:17; Deuteronomy 5:21)

Pause to add your own prayers for commitment and renewal.

Personal Concerns

O LORD, you are my refuge; never let me be disgraced. Rescue me! Save me from my enemies, for you are just. Turn your ear to listen and set me free. Be to me a protecting rock of safety, where I am always welcome. Give the order to save me, for you are my rock and my fortress. (Psalm 71:1–3)

Growth in Character

Pause to look to the Lord for the power to stand firm in the spiritual warfare against the world, the flesh, and spiritual forces of wickedness. Ask that you would grow in character and pursue the disciplines of the faith in a spirit of radical dependence upon him.

Concerns for Others

May I not forget about those in prison. May I suffer with them as though I were there myself. I will share the sorrow of those being mistreated, as though I felt their pain in my own body. (Hebrews 13:3)

World Affairs

Lift up the needs of the poor and the hungry, the oppressed and the persecuted. Pray for those in positions of authority and ask for the blessings of peace rather than conflict.

Prayer of Thanksgiving

God sent Jesus to take the punishment for our sins and to satisfy God's anger against us. We are made right with God when we believe that Jesus shed his blood, sacrificing his life for us. God was being entirely fair and just when he did not punish those who sinned in former times. And he is entirely fair and just in this present time when he declares sinners to be right in his sight because they believe in Jesus. Can we boast, then, that we have done anything to be accepted by God? No, because our acquittal is not based on our good deeds. It is based on our faith. So we are made right with God through faith and not by obeying the law. (Romans 3:25–28)

Pause to offer your own expressions of thanksgiving.

Concluding Prayer

Jesus is the one referred to in the Scriptures, where it says, "The stone that you builders rejected has now become the cornerstone." There is salvation in no one else! There is no other name in all of heaven for people to call on to save them. (Acts 4:11–12)

Jesus is the Messiah, the Son of God, and by believing in him I have life. (John 20:31)

Day 23

Praise and Worship

Exalt the LORD our God and worship at his holy mountain in Jerusalem, for the LORD our God is holy! (Psalm 99:9)

Taste and see that the LORD is good. Oh, the joys of those who trust in him! Let the LORD's people show him reverence, for those who honor him will have all they need. (Psalm 34:8–9)

Pause to express your thoughts of praise and worship.

Personal Examination

My dear children, I am writing this to you so that you will not sin. But if you do sin, there is someone to plead for you before the Father. He is Jesus Christ, the one who pleases God completely. He is the sacrifice for our sins. He takes away not only our sins but the sins of all the world. (1 John 2:1–2)

Ask the Spirit to search your heart and reveal any areas of unconfessed sin. Acknowledge these to the Lord and thank him for his forgiveness.

Commitment

May I love my enemies and do good to those who hate me. I will pray for the happiness of those who curse me and those who hurt me. May I give what I have to anyone who asks me for it; and when things are taken away from me, not try to get them back. May I do for others as I would like them to do for me. (Luke 6:27–28, 30–31)

Pause to add your own prayers for commitment and renewal.

Personal Concerns

May I live carefully, not as a fool but one who is wise. May I make the most of every opportunity for doing good in these evil days. May I not act thoughtlessly, but try to understand what the Lord wants me to do. (Ephesians 5:15–17)

Knowing, Loving, and Trusting God
Pause to ask God for the grace to know and please him. Ask him to enlarge your capacity to love him more and abide wholly in him.

Concerns for Others

Since we have been invited into this wonderful friendship with Jesus Christ our Lord, we should stop arguing and let there be real harmony so there won't be divisions in the church. We should be of one mind, united in thought and purpose. (1 Corinthians 1:9–10)

Churches and Ministries
Ask God to work on behalf of the people and concerns at your local church. Pray for his blessing and power in the ministries that are engaged in Christian witness, discipleship, education, and those serving people in need.

Prayer of Thanksgiving

Since I have been united with him in his death, I will also be raised as he was. (Romans 6:5)

We can never stop thanking God for all the generous gifts he has given us, now that we belong to Christ Jesus. He has enriched our church with the gifts of eloquence and every kind of knowledge. Now we have every spiritual gift we need as we eagerly wait for the return of our Lord Jesus Christ. (1 Corinthians 1:4–5, 7)

Pause to offer your own expressions of thanksgiving.

Concluding Prayer

God, who said, "Let there be light in the darkness," has made us understand that this light is the brightness of the glory of God that is seen in the face of Jesus Christ. But this precious treasure—this light and power that now shine within us—is held in perishable containers, that is, in our weak bodies. So everyone can see that our glorious power is from God and is not our own. (2 Corinthians 4:6–7)

Your gracious favor is all I need. Your power works best in my weakness. So now I am glad to boast about my weaknesses, so that the power of Christ may work through me. Since I know it is all for Christ's good, I am quite content with my weaknesses and with insults, hardships, persecutions, and calamities. For when I am weak, then I am strong. (2 Corinthians 12:9–10)

Day 24

Praise and Worship

Your unfailing love, O LORD, is as vast as the heavens; your faithfulness reaches beyond the clouds. Your righteousness is like the mighty mountains, your justice like the ocean depths. You care for people and animals alike, O LORD. How precious is your unfailing love, O God! All humanity finds shelter in the shadow of your wings. For you are the fountain of life, the light by which we see. (Psalm 36:5–7, 9)

I will praise God's name with singing, and I will honor him with thanksgiving. (Psalm 69:30)

Pause to express your thoughts of praise and worship.

Personal Examination

Pride goes before destruction, and haughtiness before a fall. (Proverbs 16:18)

Ask the Spirit to search your heart and reveal any areas of unconfessed sin. Acknowledge these to the Lord and thank him for his forgiveness.

Commitment

Before, I let myself be a slave of impurity and lawlessness. But now I must choose to be a slave of righteousness so that I will become holy. (Romans 6:19)

Those who are dominated by the flesh think about sinful things, but those who are controlled by the Holy Spirit think about things that please the Spirit. If your flesh controls your mind, there is death. But if the Holy Spirit controls your mind, there is life and peace. (Romans 8:5–6)

Pause to add your own prayers for commitment and renewal.

Personal Concerns

For the Lord's sake, may I accept all authority—the king as head of state, and the officials he has appointed. For the king has sent them to punish all who do wrong and to honor those who do right. It is God's will that my good life should silence those who make foolish accusations against me. (1 Peter 2:13–15)

Greater Wisdom

Pause to ask God for the grace to develop an eternal perspective on your life and concerns, and that he would renew your mind with his truth. Ask for the power to order your steps with wisdom and skill in each area of life so that you will seek to please him rather than impress others.

Concerns for Others

May we love each other with genuine affection, and take delight in honoring each other. (Romans 12:10)

Loved Ones

Lift up the members of your immediate family and your extended family. Pray for the spiritual, emotional, and physical concerns of your loved ones.

Prayer of Thanksgiving

I will not turn from the God who can save me—the Rock who can hide me. (Isaiah 17:10)

O Lord, I will honor and praise your name, for you are my God. You do such wonderful things! You planned them long ago, and now you have accomplished them. (Isaiah 25:1)

Pause to offer your own expressions of thanksgiving.

Concluding Prayer

When I tried to keep the law, I realized I could never earn God's approval. So I died to the law so that I might live for God. I have been crucified with Christ. I myself no longer live, but Christ lives in me. So I live my life in this earthly body by trusting in the Son of God, who loved me and gave himself for me. (Galatians 2:19–20)

To me, living is for Christ, and dying is even better. (Philippians 1:21)

Day 25

Praise and Worship

You are God, O Sovereign LORD. Your words are truth, and you have promised these good things to me, your servant. (2 Samuel 7:28)

I will sing of your love and justice. I will praise you, LORD, with songs. (Psalm 101:1)

Pause to express your thoughts of praise and worship.

Personal Examination

There is not a single person in all the earth who is always good and never sins. (Ecclesiastes 7:20)

Ask the Spirit to search your heart and reveal any areas of unconfessed sin. Acknowledge these to the Lord and thank him for his forgiveness.

Commitment

May I get rid of all bitterness, rage, anger, harsh words, and slander, as well as all types of malicious behavior. Instead, may I be kind to others, tenderhearted, and forgiving, just as God through Christ has forgiven me. (Ephesians 4:31–32)

In everything I do, may I stay away from complaining and arguing, so that no one can speak a word of blame against me. I am to live a clean, innocent life as a child of God in a dark world full of crooked and perverse people. Let my life shine brightly before them. May I hold tightly to the word of life, so that when Christ returns, I will be proud that I did not lose the race and that my work was not useless. (Philippians 2:14–16)

Pause to add your own prayers for commitment and renewal.

Personal Concerns

May I not be afraid of the enemy! I remember the Lord, who is great and glorious, and I fight for my friends, my family, and my home! (Nehemiah 4:14)

Spiritual Insight
Pause to ask that the Holy Spirit would give you understanding and insight into the word of truth, so that you will have a growing grasp of your identity in Christ—where you came from, who you are, and where you are going. Ask for a clearer understanding of God's purpose for your life.

Concerns for Others

We are careful to be honorable before the Lord, but we also want everyone else to know we are honorable. (2 Corinthians 8:21)

Other Believers
Intercede in the lives of your personal friends, and ask that the Lord will bless their families, their careers, and their ministries. Pray that he will comfort and strengthen those who are oppressed and in need.

Prayer of Thanksgiving

You let Pharoah live —that he might see your power
and that your fame might spread throughout the earth.
(Exodus 9:16)

God can turn into good what others mean for evil.
(Genesis 50:20)

Pause to offer your own expressions of thanksgiving.

Concluding Prayer

How great is our LORD! His power is absolute! His understanding is beyond comprehension. (Psalm 147:5)

Reverence for the LORD is the foundation of true wisdom. The rewards of wisdom come to all who obey
him. Praise his name forever! (Psalm 111:10)

Day 26

Praise and Worship

The LORD Almighty is a wonderful teacher, and he gives great wisdom. (Isaiah 28:29)

You are the LORD, and there is no other Savior. From eternity to eternity you are God. No one can oppose what you do. No one can reverse your actions. (Isaiah 43:11, 13)

Pause to express your thoughts of praise and worship.

Personal Examination

You will bless those who have humble and contrite hearts, who tremble at my word. (Isaiah 66:2b)

Ask the Spirit to search your heart and reveal any areas of unconfessed sin. Acknowledge these to the Lord and thank him for his forgiveness.

Commitment

If I have found favor with you, show me your intentions so I will understand you more fully and do exactly what you want me to do. (Exodus 33:13)

May I set myself apart to be holy, for you, the LORD, are my God. May I keep all your laws and obey them, for you are the LORD, who makes me holy. (Leviticus 20:7–8)

Pause to add your own prayers for commitment and renewal.

Personal Concerns

LORD, I have come to you for protection; don't let me be put to shame. Rescue me, for you always do what is right. You are my rock and my fortress. For the honor of your name, lead me out of this peril. I entrust my spirit into your hand. Rescue me, LORD, for you are a faithful God. (Psalm 31:1, 3, 5)

Love and Compassion
Pause to ask for the grace of greater love and compassion for others. Pray that you will become a more Christlike person who considers the needs of others above your own, knowing that God is your provider and sustainer.

Concerns for Others

May I worship Christ as Lord of my life. And if I am asked about my Christian hope, I will always be ready to explain it. (1 Peter 3:15)

Christian Witness
Pray on behalf of the people you personally know who have not yet entered into the joy of a personal relationship with Jesus. Intercede for your unsaved relatives, neighbors, co-workers, and friends.

Prayer of Thanksgiving

I was dead because of my sins and because my flesh was not yet cut away. Then God made me alive with Christ. He forgave all my sins. He canceled the record that contained the charges against me. He took it and destroyed it by nailing it to Christ's cross. In this way, God disarmed the evil rulers and authorities. He shamed them publicly by his victory over them on the cross of Christ. (Colossians 2:13–15)

God decided to save us through our Lord Jesus Christ, not to pour out his anger on us. He died for us so that we can live with him forever, whether we are dead or alive at the time of his return. (1 Thessalonians 5:9–10)

Pause to offer your own expressions of thanksgiving.

Concluding Prayer

All praise to the God and Father of our Lord Jesus Christ. He is the source of every mercy and the God who comforts us. (2 Corinthians 1:3)

I pray that God, who gives you hope, will keep you happy and full of peace as you believe in him. May you overflow with hope through the power of the Holy Spirit. (Romans 15:13)

Day 27

Praise and Worship

Will God really live on earth? Why, even the highest heavens cannot contain you. How much less this Temple I have built! (1 Kings 8:27)

God's voice is glorious in the thunder. We cannot comprehend the greatness of his power. (Job 37:5)

Pause to express your thoughts of praise and worship.

Personal Examination

He was despised and rejected—a man of sorrows, acquainted with bitterest grief. We turned our backs on him and looked the other way when he went by. He was despised, and we did not care. Yet it was our weaknesses he carried; it was our sorrows that weighed him down. And we thought his troubles were a punishment from God for his own sins!

But he was wounded and crushed for our sins. He was beaten that we might have peace. He was whipped, and we were healed! All of us have strayed away like sheep. We have left God's paths to follow our own. Yet the LORD laid on him the guilt and sins of us all. (Isaiah 53:3–6)

Ask the Spirit to search your heart and reveal any areas of unconfessed sin. Acknowledge these to the Lord and thank him for his forgiveness.

Commitment

You must be holy because I, the LORD, am holy. I have set you apart from all other people to be my very own. (Leviticus 20:26)

May I learn to fear you as long as I live on the earth and teach your words to my children. (Deuteronomy 4:10)

May I be careful and beware that in my plenty I do not forget the LORD my God and disobey his commands, regulations, and laws. (Deuteronomy 8:11)

Pause to add your own prayers for commitment and renewal.

Personal Concerns

Just as I accepted Christ Jesus as my Lord, I must continue to live in obedience to him. May I let my roots grow down into him and draw up nourishment from him, so I will grow in faith, strong and vigorous in the truth I was taught. Let my life overflow with thanksgiving for all he has done. (Colossians 2:6–7)

Faithfulness as a Steward

Pause to ask that God would empower you to become a more faithful and effective steward with all that he has entrusted to your care. Since he has given you a stewardship of talents, treasure, truth, time, and love and compassion, ask that you would use these gifts with fidelity in his service.

Concerns for Others

We should pray for all people. As we make our requests, we plead for God's mercy upon them, and give thanks.

We pray this way for kings and all others who are in authority, so that we can live in peace and quietness, in godliness and dignity. This is good and pleases God our Savior, for he wants everyone to be saved and to understand the truth. (1 Timothy 2:1–4)

Government

Lift up those in local, state, and national government, and pray that those in positions of authority would look to God for wisdom in their decisions and practice.

Prayer of Thanksgiving

This is a true saying, and everyone should believe it: Christ Jesus came into the world to save sinners—and I was the worst of them all. But that is why God had mercy on me, so that Christ Jesus could use me as a prime example of his great patience with even the worst sinners. Then others will realize that they, too, can believe in him and receive eternal life. (1 Timothy 1:15–16)

God has saved me and chose me to live a holy life. He did this not because I deserved it, but because that was his plan long before the world began—to show his love and kindness to us through Christ Jesus. (2 Timothy 1:9)

Pause to offer your own expressions of thanksgiving.

Concluding Prayer

For you are my hiding place; you protect me from trouble. You surround me with songs of victory. (Psalm 32:7)

The LORD says, "I will guide you along the best pathway for your life. I will advise you and watch over you." (Psalm 32:8)

Day 28

Praise and Worship

True wisdom and power are with you; counsel and understanding are yours. (Job 12:13)

You are holy. The praises of Israel surround your throne. (Psalm 22:3)

Pause to express your thoughts of praise and worship.

Personal Examination

People may be pure in their own eyes, but the LORD examines their motives. (Proverbs 16:2)

Ask the Spirit to search your heart and reveal any areas of unconfessed sin. Acknowledge these to the Lord and thank him for his forgiveness.

Commitment

May I always be joyful and keep on praying. No matter what happens, I will always be thankful, for this is God's will for me, because I belong to him. (1 Thessalonians 5:16–18)

I can really know Christ and experience the mighty power that raised him from the dead. I can learn what it means to suffer with him, sharing in his death, so that, somehow, I can experience the resurrection from the dead! (Philippians 3:10–11)

Pause to add your own prayers for commitment and renewal.

Personal Concerns

You deal well with me, O Sovereign LORD, for the sake of your own reputation! Rescue me because you are so faithful and good. (Psalm 109:21)

Family and Ministry

Pause to lift up your family, your career, and your ministry before the Lord. Ask that you would have the privilege of sharing Christ with others and helping people grow in their knowledge of him.

Concerns for Others

May God be merciful and bless us. May his face shine with favor upon us. May your ways be known throughout the earth, your saving power among people everywhere. (Psalm 67:1–2)

Missions

Intercede for national and world missions, and pray that those who have dedicated their lives to the fulfillment of the Great Commission will be strengthened, encouraged, and empowered.

Prayer of Thanksgiving

When God our Savior showed us his kindness and love, he saved us, not because of the good things we did, but because of his mercy. He washed away our sins and gave us a new life through the Holy Spirit. He generously poured out the Spirit upon us because of what Jesus Christ our Savior did. He declared us not guilty because of his great kindness. And now we know that we will inherit eternal life. (Titus 3:4–7)

My hope in God is like a strong and trustworthy anchor for my soul. It leads me through the curtain of heaven into God's inner sanctuary. (Hebrews 6:19–20)

Pause to offer your own expressions of thanksgiving.

Concluding Prayer

I have seen you in your sanctuary and gazed upon your power and glory. Your unfailing love is better to me than life itself; how I praise you! I will honor you as long as I live, lifting up my hands to you in prayer. You satisfy me more than the richest of foods. I will praise you with songs of joy. (Psalm 63:2–5)

Glory be to God! By his mighty power at work within us, he is able to accomplish infinitely more than we would ever dare to ask or hope. May he be given glory in the church and in Christ Jesus forever and ever through endless ages. Amen. (Ephesians 3:20–21)

Day 29

Praise and Worship

You, O Lord, are a merciful and gracious God, slow to get angry, full of unfailing love and truth. (Psalm 86:15)

I tremble in fear of you; I fear your judgments. (Psalm 119:120)

Pause to express your thoughts of praise and worship.

Personal Examination

From the depths of despair, O Lord, I call for your help. Hear my cry, O Lord. Pay attention to my prayer. Lord, if you kept a record of our sins, who, O Lord, could ever survive? But you offer forgiveness, that we might learn to fear you. (Psalm 130:1–4)

Ask the Spirit to search your heart and reveal any areas of unconfessed sin. Acknowledge these to the Lord and thank him for his forgiveness.

Commitment

Give me wisdom and knowledge to rule properly, for who is able to govern this great nation of yours? God said to Solomon, "Because your greatest desire is to help your people, and you did not ask for personal wealth and honor or the death of your enemies or even a long life, but rather you asked for wisdom and knowledge to properly govern my people, I will certainly give you the wisdom and knowledge you requested. And I will also give you riches, wealth, and honor such as no other king has ever had before you or will ever have again!" (2 Chronicles 1:10–12)

May I not be upset over details! There is really only one thing worth being concerned about. Like Mary, may I discover the good part that won't be taken away from me. (Luke 10:41–42)

Pause to add your own prayers for commitment and renewal.

Personal Concerns

Answer my prayers, O LORD, for your unfailing love is wonderful. Turn and take care of me, for your mercy is so plentiful. (Psalm 69:16)

Growth in Character
Pause to look to the Lord for the power to stand firm in the spiritual warfare against the world, the flesh, and spiritual forces of wickedness. Ask that you would grow in character and pursue the disciplines of the faith in a spirit of radical dependence upon him.

Concerns for Others

O LORD, you are a great and awesome God! You always fulfill your promises of unfailing love to those who love you and keep your commands. But we have sinned and done wrong. We have rebelled against you and scorned your commands and regulations. But you are merciful and forgiving, even though we have rebelled against you. We have not obeyed you, for we have not followed the laws you gave us through your servants the prophets. (Daniel 9:4–5, 9–10)

World Affairs

Lift up the needs of the poor and the hungry, the oppressed and the persecuted. Pray for those in positions of authority and ask for the blessings of peace rather than conflict.

Prayer of Thanksgiving

I love him even though I have never seen him. Though I do not see him, I trust him; and even now I am happy with a glorious, inexpressible joy. My reward for trusting him will be the salvation of my soul. (1 Peter 1:8–9)

Since I am receiving a Kingdom that cannot be destroyed, let me be thankful and please you by worshipping you with holy fear and awe. For my God is a consuming fire. (Hebrews 12:28–29)

Pause to offer your own expressions of thanksgiving.

Concluding Prayer

The Father has enabled me to share the inheritance that belongs to God's holy people, who live in the light. For he has rescued me from the one who rules in the kingdom of darkness, and he has brought me into the Kingdom of his dear Son. God has purchased my freedom with his blood and has forgiven all my sins. (Colossians 1:12–14)

It is my aim to please him always, whether I am here in this body or away from this body. For I must stand before Christ to be judged. I will receive whatever I deserve for the good or evil I have done in my body. (2 Corinthians 5:9–10)

Day 30

Praise and Worship

Each of these living beings had six wings, and their wings were covered with eyes, inside and out. Day after day and night after night they keep on saying, "Holy, holy, holy is the Lord God Almighty—the one who always was, who is, and who is still to come." (Revelation 4:8)

From the throne came a voice that said, "Praise our God, all his servants, from the least to the greatest, all who fear him." (Revelation 19:5)

Pause to express your thoughts of praise and worship.

Personal Examination

I have sinned greatly and shouldn't have. Please forgive me, Lord, for doing this foolish thing. (2 Samuel 24:10)

Ask the Spirit to search your heart and reveal any areas of unconfessed sin. Acknowledge these to the Lord and thank him for his forgiveness.

Commitment

When I obey you, I should say, "I am not worthy of praise. I am a servant who has simply done my duty." (Luke 17:10)

May I carry out the tasks assigned me by the one who sent me, because there is little time left before the night falls and all work comes to an end. (John 9:4)

Pause to add your own prayers for commitment and renewal.

Personal Concerns

I have tried my best to find you—don't let me wander from your commands. (Psalm 119:10)

Knowing, Loving, and Trusting God

Pause to ask God for the grace to know and please him. Ask him to enlarge your capacity to love him more and abide wholly in him.

Concerns for Others

Pure and lasting religion in the sight of God our Father means that we must care for orphans and widows in their troubles, and refuse to let the world corrupt us. (James 1:27)

Churches and Ministries

Ask God to work on behalf of the people and concerns at your local church. Pray for his blessing and power in the ministries that are engaged in Christian witness, discipleship, education, and those serving people in need.

Prayer of Thanksgiving

You gave me life and showed me your unfailing love. My life was preserved by your care. (Job 10:12)

God is my shield, saving those whose hearts are true and right. (Psalm 7:10)

I am overcome with joy because of your unfailing love, for you have seen my troubles, and you care about the anguish of my soul. (Psalm 31:7)

Pause to offer your own expressions of thanksgiving.

Concluding Prayer

Give honor to the LORD, you angels; give honor to the LORD for his glory and strength. Give honor to the LORD for the glory of his name. Worship the LORD in the splendor of his holiness. (Psalm 29:1–2)

Glory and honor to God forever and ever. He is the eternal King, the unseen one who never dies; he alone is God. Amen. (1 Timothy 1:17)

Day 31

Praise and Worship

The LORD is king! He is robed in majesty. Indeed, the LORD is robed in majesty and armed with strength. The world is firmly established; it cannot be shaken. Your throne, O LORD, has been established from time immemorial. You yourself are from the everlasting past. Your royal decrees cannot be changed. The nature of your reign, O LORD, is holiness forever. (Psalm 93:1–2, 5)

God sits above the circle of the earth. The people below must seem to him like grasshoppers! He is the one who spreads out the heavens like a curtain and makes his tent from them. He judges the great people of the world and brings them all to nothing. (Isaiah 40:22–23)

Pause to express your thoughts of praise and worship.

Personal Examination

God carefully watches the way people live; he sees everything they do. No darkness is thick enough to hide the wicked from his eyes. For it is not up to mortals to decide when to come before God in judgment. (Job 34:21–23)

Ask the Spirit to search your heart and reveal any areas of unconfessed sin. Acknowledge these to the Lord and thank him for his forgiveness.

Commitment

May I never reject this marvelous message of God's great kindness. For God says, "At just the right time, I heard you. On the day of salvation, I helped you." Indeed, God is ready to help me right now. Today is the day of salvation. (2 Corinthians 6:1–2)

Please make my heart strong, blameless, and holy when I stand before you on that day when our Lord Jesus comes with all those who belong to him. (1 Thessalonians 3:13)

Pause to add your own prayers for commitment and renewal.

Personal Concerns

O LORD, I am calling to you. Please hurry! Listen when I cry to you for help! Accept my prayer as incense offered to you, and my upraised hands as an evening offering. (Psalm 141:1–2)

Greater Wisdom

Pause to ask God for the grace to develop an eternal perspective on your life and concerns, and that he would renew your mind with his truth. Ask for the power to order your steps with wisdom and skill in each area of life so that you will seek to please him rather than impress others.

Concerns for Others

You have called us to go and make disciples of all the nations, baptizing them in the name of the Father and the Son and the Holy Spirit and teaching these new disciples to obey all the commands you have given. I am sure of this: you are with me always, even to the end of the age. (Matthew 28:19–20)

Loved Ones

Lift up the members of your immediate family and your extended family. Pray for the spiritual, emotional, and physical concerns of your loved ones.

Prayer of Thanksgiving

The LORD will demonstrate his holy power before the eyes of all the nations. The ends of the earth will see the salvation of our God. (Isaiah 52:10)

His mighty arm does tremendous things! How he scatters the proud and haughty ones! He has taken princes from their thrones and exalted the lowly. (Luke 1:51–52)

Pause to offer your own expressions of thanksgiving.

Concluding Prayer

I am not ashamed, for I know the one in whom I trust, and I am sure that he is able to guard what I have entrusted to him until the day of his return. (2 Timothy 1:12)

And now, may the God of peace, who brought again from the dead our Lord Jesus, equip me with all I need for doing his will. May he produce in me, through the power of Jesus Christ, all that is pleasing to him. Jesus is the great Shepherd of the sheep by an everlasting covenant, signed with his blood. To him be glory forever and ever. Amen. (Hebrews 13:20–21)

One-Week Prayer Guide

Sunday

Praise and Worship

Not to us, O Lord, but to you goes all the glory for your unfailing love and faithfulness. (Psalm 115:1)

It is good to give thanks to the Lord, to sing praises to the Most High. It is good to proclaim your unfailing love in the morning, your faithfulness in the evening. (Psalm 92:1–2)

Great and marvelous are your actions, Lord God Almighty. Just and true are your ways, O King of the nations. Who will not fear, O Lord, and glorify your name? For you alone are holy. All nations will come and worship before you, for your righteous deeds have been revealed. (Revelation 15:3–4)

Sing a new song to the Lord! Let the whole earth sing to the Lord! Sing to the Lord; bless his name. Each day proclaim the good news that he saves. Publish his glorious deeds among the nations. Tell everyone about the amazing things he does. Great is the Lord! He is most worthy of praise! He is to be revered above all the gods. The gods of other nations are merely idols, but the Lord made the heavens! Honor and majesty surround him; strength and beauty are in his sanctuary. (Psalm 96:1–6)

Pause to express your thoughts of praise and worship.

Personal Examination

You will bless those who have humble and contrite hearts, who tremble at your word. (Isaiah 66:2b)

What is more pleasing to the LORD: sacrifices or obedience to his voice? Obedience is far better than sacrifice. Listening to him is much better. (1 Samuel 15:22)

The sacrifice you want is a broken spirit. A broken and repentant heart, O God, you will not despise. (Psalm 51:17)

If I confess my sins to him, he is faithful and just to forgive me and to cleanse me from every wrong. (1 John 1:9)

The LORD doesn't make decisions the way we do! People judge by outward appearance, but the LORD looks at a person's thoughts and intentions. (1 Samuel 16:7)

Thank you that you have said:

Come now, let us argue this out. No matter how deep the stain of your sins, I can remove it. I can make you as clean as freshly fallen snow. Even if you are stained as red as crimson, I can make you as white as wool. (Isaiah 1:18)

Ask the Spirit to search your heart and reveal any areas of unconfessed sin. Acknowledge these to the Lord and thank him for his forgiveness.

Commitment

Lord, renew me by your Spirit as I offer these prayers to you:

By your grace, I want to hear the words, "Well done, my good and faithful servant. You have been faithful in handling this small amount, so now I will give you many more responsibilities. Let's celebrate together!' (Matthew 25:21)

May I be careful to live a blameless life—when will you come to my aid? I will lead a life of integrity in my own home. I will refuse to look at anything vile and vulgar. I hate all crooked dealings; I will have nothing to do with them. (Psalm 101:2–3)

May I throw off my old evil nature and my former way of life, which is rotten through and through, full of lust and deception. Instead, there must be a spiritual renewal of my thoughts and attitudes. May I display a new nature because I am a new person, created in God's likeness—righteous, holy, and true. (Ephesians 4:22–24)

May I set myself apart to be holy, for you, the LORD, are my God. May I keep all your laws and obey them, for you are the LORD, who makes me holy. (Leviticus 20:7–8)

Pause to add your own prayers for personal renewal.

Personal Concerns

Father, using your Word as a guide, I offer you my prayers concerning dedication to you.

Since I have been raised to new life with Christ, may I set my sights on the realities of heaven, where Christ sits at God's right hand in the place of honor and power. I will let heaven fill my thoughts. I will not think only about things down here on earth. For I died when Christ died, and my real life is hidden with Christ in God. And when Christ, who is my real life, is revealed to the whole world, I will share in all his glory. (Colossians 3:1–4)

May I give my body to God, letting it be a living and holy sacrifice—the kind he will accept. When I think of what he has done for me, is this too much to ask? May I not copy the behavior and customs of this world, but let God transform me into a new person by changing the way I think. Then I will know what God wants me to do, and I will know how good and pleasing and perfect his will really is. (Romans 12:1–2)

May I break down every proud argument that keeps people from knowing God. With these weapons we conquer their rebellious ideas, and we teach them to obey Christ. (2 Corinthians 10:5)

If anyone refuses to take up their cross and follow you, they are not worthy of being yours. If anyone clings to his life, he will lose it; but if he gives it up for you, he will find it. (Matthew 10:38–39)

313

Trust in the LORD and do good. Then you will live safely in the land and prosper. Take delight in the LORD, and he will give you your heart's desires. Commit everything you do to the LORD. Trust him, and he will help you. He will make your innocence as clear as the dawn, and the justice of your cause will shine like the noonday sun. (Psalm 37:3–6)

Come, my children, and listen to me, and I will teach you to fear the LORD. Do any of you want to live a life that is long and good? Then watch your tongue! Keep your lips from telling lies! Turn away from evil and do good. Work hard at living in peace with others. The eyes of the LORD watch over those who do right; his ears are open to their cries for help. (Psalm 34:11–15)

Show me the path where I should walk, O LORD; point out the right road for me to follow. Lead me by your truth and teach me, for you are the God who saves me. All day long I put my hope in you. Remember, O LORD, your unfailing love and compassion, which you have shown from long ages past. (Psalm 25:4–6)

And now, Israel, what does the LORD your God require of you? He requires you to fear him, to live according to his will, to love and worship him with all your heart and soul. (Deuteronomy 10:12)

Our Father in heaven, may your name be honored. May your Kingdom come soon. May your will be done here on earth, just as it is in heaven. Give us our food for today, and forgive us our sins, just as we have forgiven those who have sinned against us. And don't let us yield to temptation, but deliver us from the evil one. (Matthew 6:9–13)

Pause here to express any additional personal requests, especially concerning growth in Christ:

Greater desire to know and please him
Greater love and commitment to him
Grace to practice his presence
Grace to glorify him in my life
My activities for this day
Special concerns

Concerns for Others

Lord, I now prepare my heart for intercessory prayer for churches and ministries.

May our Lord Jesus Christ and God our Father, who loved us and in his special favor gave us everlasting comfort and good hope, comfort our hearts and give us strength in every good thing we do and say. (2 Thessalonians 2:16–17)

We should share each other's troubles and problems, and in this way obey the law of Christ. (Galatians 6:2)

Confess your sins to each other and pray for each other so that you may be healed. The earnest prayer of a righteous person has great power and wonderful results. (James 5:16)

In the spirit of these passages, I pray for:

My local church
Other churches
Christian witness and discipleship ministries
Educational ministries
Special concerns

Prayer of Thanksgiving

For who you are and for what you have done, accept my thanks, O Lord:

I am overwhelmed with joy in the LORD my God! For he has dressed me with the clothing of salvation and draped me in a robe of righteousness. I am like a bridegroom in his wedding suit or a bride with her jewels. (Isaiah 61:10)

I wait quietly before God, for my salvation comes from him. He alone is my rock and my salvation, my fortress where I will never be shaken. (Psalm 62:1–2)

I will lie down in peace and sleep, for you alone, O LORD, will keep me safe. (Psalm 4:8)

These are the words he sang: "The LORD is my rock, my fortress, and my savior; my God is my rock, in whom I find protection. He is my shield, the strength of my salvation, and my stronghold, my high tower, my savior, the one who saves me from violence." (2 Samuel 22:2–3)

Pause to offer your own expressions of thanksgiving.

Concluding Prayer

Satisfy us in the morning with your unfailing love, so we may sing for joy to the end of our lives. (Psalm 90:14)

In his kindness God called me to his eternal glory by means of Jesus Christ. After I have suffered a little while, he will restore, support, and strengthen me, and he will place me on a firm foundation. All power is his forever and ever. Amen. (1 Peter 5:10–11)

And now, all glory to you, who are able to keep me from stumbling, and who will bring me into your glorious presence innocent of sin and with great joy. All glory to you, who alone are God and Savior, through Jesus Christ my Lord. Yes, glory, majesty, power, and authority belong to you, in the beginning, now, and forevermore. Amen. (Jude 24–25)

Monday

Praise and Worship

I will praise you, my God and King, and bless your name forever and ever. I will bless you every day, and I will praise you forever. Great is the LORD! He is most worthy of praise! His greatness is beyond discovery! Let each generation tell its children of your mighty acts. I will meditate on your majestic, glorious splendor and your wonderful miracles. Your awe-inspiring deeds will be on every tongue; I will proclaim your greatness. Everyone will share the story of your wonderful goodness; they will sing with joy of your righteousness. The LORD is kind and merciful, slow to get angry, full of unfailing love. The LORD is good to everyone. He showers compassion on all his creation. (Psalm 145:1–9)

O LORD, our LORD, the majesty of your name fills the earth! Your glory is higher than the heavens! (Psalm 8:1)

You are both the source of David and the heir to his throne. You are the bright morning star. (Revelation 22:16)

Bless the LORD God, the God of Israel, who alone does such wonderful things. Bless his glorious name forever! Let the whole earth be filled with his glory. Amen and amen! (Psalm 72:18–19)

Pause to express your thoughts of praise and worship.

Personal Examination

He was wounded and crushed for our sins. He was beaten that we might have peace. He was whipped, and we were healed! All of us have strayed away like sheep. We have left God's paths to follow our own. Yet the LORD laid on him the guilt and sins of us all. (Isaiah 53:5–6)

Turn to me now, while there is time! Give me your hearts. Come with fasting, weeping, and mourning. Don't tear your clothing in your grief; instead, tear your hearts, says the LORD. Return to the LORD your God, for he is gracious and merciful. He is not easily angered. He is filled with kindness and is eager not to punish you. (Joel 2:12–13)

The LORD is close to the brokenhearted; he rescues those who are crushed in spirit. (Psalm 34:18)

I have heard all about you, LORD, and I am filled with awe by the amazing things you have done. In this time of my deep need, begin again to help me, as you did in years gone by. Show me your power to save me. And in your anger, remember your mercy. (Habakkuk 3:2)

Ask the Spirit to search your heart and reveal any areas of unconfessed sin. Acknowledge these to the Lord and thank him for his forgiveness.

Thank you, LORD, that you have said: "For a brief moment I abandoned you, but with great compassion I will take you back. In a moment of anger I turned my face away for a little while. But with everlasting love I will have compassion on you." (Isaiah 54:7–8)

Commitment

Lord, renew me by your Spirit as I offer these prayers to you:

May I obey the commands of the LORD my God by walking in his ways and fearing him, serving only you and fearing you alone. May I obey your commands, listen to your voice, and cling to you. (Deuteronomy 8:6; 13:4)

May I worship and serve you with my whole heart and with a willing mind. For you, LORD, see every heart and understand and know every plan and thought. If I seek you, I will find you. But if I forsake you, you will reject me forever. (1 Chronicles 28:9)

May I love the LORD my God with all my heart and soul, and worship him. (Deuteronomy 11:13)

May I love my enemies and do good to those who hate me. I will pray for the happiness of those who curse me and those who hurt me. May I give what I have to anyone who asks me for it; and when things are taken away from me, not try to get them back. May I do for others as I would like them to do for me. (Luke 6:27–28, 30–31)

Pause to add your own prayers for personal renewal.

Personal Concerns

Father, using your Word as a guide, I offer you my prayers concerning the things of the world. May these beatitudes be a reality in my life:

God blesses those who realize their need for him, for the Kingdom of Heaven is given to them. God blesses those who mourn, for they will be comforted. God blesses those who are gentle and lowly, for the whole earth will belong to them. God blesses those who are hungry and thirsty for justice, for they will receive it in full. God blesses those who are merciful, for they will be shown mercy. God blesses those whose hearts are pure, for they will see God. God blesses those who work for peace, for they will be called the children of God. God blesses those who are persecuted because they live for God, for the Kingdom of Heaven is theirs. (Matthew 5:3–10)

You will give me all I need from day to day if I live for you and make the Kingdom of God my primary concern. (Matthew 6:33)

When I discover a pearl of great value, may I sell everything I own to buy it! (Matthew 13:46)

Make me walk along the path of your commands, for that is where my happiness is found. Give me an eagerness for your decrees; do not inflict me with love for money! Turn my eyes from worthless things, and give me life through your word. (Psalm 119:36–37)

May I stay away from the love of money and be satisfied with what I have. For you have said, "I will never fail you. I will never forsake you." (Hebrews 13:5)

May I not be like the thorny ground, which represents those who hear and accept the Good News, but all too quickly the message is crowded out by the cares of this life and the lure of wealth, so no crop is produced. Instead, may I be like the good soil, which represents the hearts of those who truly accept God's message and produce a huge harvest—thirty, sixty, or even a hundred times as much as had been planted. (Matthew 13:22–23; Mark 4:18–20; Luke 8:14–15)

As a servant of Christ who has been put in charge of explaining God's secrets and as a manager, I must be faithful. (1 Corinthians 4:1–2)

No one can serve two masters. For you will hate one and love the other, or be devoted to one and despise the other. You cannot serve both God and money. (Matthew 6:24; Luke 16:13)

By your grace, I want to hear the words, "Well done, my good and faithful servant. You have been faithful in handling this small amount, so now I will give you many more responsibilities. Let's celebrate together!" (Matthew 25:21)

God forbid that I should boast about anything except the cross of our Lord Jesus Christ. Because of that cross, my interest in this world died long ago, and the world's interest in me is also long dead. (Galatians 6:14)

Lord, remind me how brief my time on earth will be. Remind me that my days are numbered, and that my life is fleeing away. (Psalm 39:4)

Teach me to make the most of my time, so that I may grow in wisdom. (Psalm 90:12)

May the Lord our God show us his approval and make our efforts successful. Yes, make our efforts successful! (Psalm 90:17)

Pause here to express any additional requests, especially concerning growth in wisdom:

Developing an eternal perspective
Renewing my mind with truth
Greater skill in each area of life
My activities for this day
Special concerns

Concerns for Others

Lord, I now prepare my heart for intercessory prayer for my family.

May the Lord make my love grow and overflow to other Christians and unbelievers. As a result, please make my heart strong, blameless, and holy when I stand before you on that day when our Lord Jesus comes with all those who belong to him. (1 Thessalonians 3:12–13)

I must commit myself wholeheartedly to the commands you give me. I will repeat them again and again to my children. I will talk about them when I am at home and when I am away on a journey, when I am lying down and when I am getting up again. (Deuteronomy 6:6–7)

In the spirit of these passages, I pray for:

My immediate family
My relatives
Spiritual concerns
Emotional and physical concerns
Other concerns

Prayer of Thanksgiving

For who you are and for what you have done, accept my thanks, Lord:

Praise the LORD, I tell myself; with my whole heart, I will praise his holy name. Praise the LORD, I tell myself, and never forget the good things he does for me. He forgives all my sins and heals all my diseases. He ransoms me from death and surrounds me with love and tender mercies. He fills my life with good things. My youth is renewed like the eagle's! (Psalm 103:1–5)

I give thanks to the LORD, for he is good! His faithful love endures forever. (1 Chronicles 16:34)

For who is God except the LORD? Who but our God is a solid rock? God is my strong fortress; he has made my way safe. He makes me as surefooted as a deer, leading me safely along the mountain heights. (2 Samuel 22:32–34)

I will give thanks to the LORD, for he is good! His faithful love endures forever. I praise the LORD for his great love and for all his wonderful deeds to them. (Psalm 107:1, 8)

Pause to offer your own expressions of thanksgiving.

Concluding Prayer

This is the day the LORD has made. We will rejoice and be glad in it. (Psalm 118:24)

May the grace of our Lord Jesus Christ, the love of God, and the fellowship of the Holy Spirit be with us all. (2 Corinthians 13:13)

God is able to make you strong, just as the Good News says. It is the message about Jesus Christ and his plan for you Gentiles, a plan kept secret from the beginning of time. But now as the prophets foretold and as the eternal God has commanded, this message is made known to all Gentiles everywhere, so that they might believe and obey Christ. To God, who alone is wise, be the glory forever through Jesus Christ. Amen. (Romans 16:25–27)

Tuesday

Praise and Worship

I will praise the LORD at all times. I will constantly speak his praises. I will boast only in the LORD; let all who are discouraged take heart. Come, let us tell of the LORD's greatness; let us exalt his name together. (Psalm 34:1–3)

Let the godly sing with joy to the LORD, for it is fitting to praise him. (Psalm 33:1)

I will keep on hoping for you to help me; I will praise you more and more. I will tell everyone about your righteousness. All day long I will proclaim your saving power, for I am overwhelmed by how much you have done for me. I will praise your mighty deeds, O Sovereign LORD. I will tell everyone that you alone are just and good. O God, you have taught me from my earliest childhood, and I have constantly told others about the wonderful things you do. (Psalm 71:14–17)

Shout with joy to the LORD, O earth! Worship the LORD with gladness. Come before him, singing with joy. Acknowledge that the LORD is God! He made us, and we are his. We are his people, the sheep of his pasture. I will enter his gates with thanksgiving; go into his courts with praise. I will give thanks to him and bless his name. For the LORD is good. His unfailing love continues forever, and his faithfulness continues to each generation. (Psalm 100:1–5)

Pause to express your thoughts of praise and worship.

Personal Examination

Have mercy on me, O God, because of your unfailing love. Because of your great compassion, blot out the stain of my sins. Wash me clean from my guilt. Purify me from my sin. For I recognize my shameful deeds—they haunt me day and night. Against you, and you alone, have I sinned; I have done what is evil in your sight. You will be proved right in what you say, and your judgment against me is just. (Psalm 51:1–4)

How can I know all the sins lurking in my heart? Cleanse me from these hidden faults. Keep me from deliberate sins! Don't let them control me. Then I will be free of guilt and innocent of great sin. (Psalm 19:12–13)

Ask the Spirit to search your heart and reveal any areas of unconfessed sin. Acknowledge these to the Lord and thank him for his forgiveness.

Purify me from my sins, and I will be clean; wash me, and I will be whiter than snow. Oh, give me back my joy again; you have broken me—now let me rejoice. Don't keep looking at my sins. Remove the stain of my guilt. Create in me a clean heart, O God. Renew a right spirit within me. Do not banish me from your presence, and don't take your Holy Spirit from me. Restore to me again the joy of your salvation, and make me willing to obey you. Then I will teach your ways to sinners, and they will return to you. (Psalm 51:7–13)

Commitment

Lord, renew me by your Spirit as I offer these prayers to you:

May I come back to my God! I will act on the principles of love and justice, and always live in confident dependence on my God. (Hosea 12:6)

May I rejoice when I run into problems and trials, for I know that they are good for me—they help me learn to endure. And endurance develops strength of character in me, and character strengthens my confident expectation of salvation. And this expectation will not disappoint me. For I know how dearly God loves me, because he has given me the Holy Spirit to fill my heart with his love. (Romans 5:3–5)

May I be glad for all God is planning for me. I will be patient in trouble, and always be prayerful. (Romans 12:12)

May I not get tired of doing what is good and not get discouraged and give up, for we will reap a harvest of blessing at the appropriate time. (Galatians 6:9)

Pause to add your own prayers for personal renewal.

Personal Concerns

Father, using your Word as a guide, I offer you my prayers concerning growth in holiness.

If I stay joined to you and your words remain in me, I may ask any request I like, and it will be granted! May I produce much fruit and bring great glory to the Father. You have loved me even as the Father has loved you. May I remain in your love. When I obey you, I remain in your love, just as you obey your Father and remain in his love. (John 15:7–11)

Search me, O God, and know my heart; test me and know my thoughts. Point out anything in me that offends you, and lead me along the path of everlasting life. (Psalm 139:23–24)

Take control of what I say, O LORD, and keep my lips sealed. Don't let me lust for evil things. (Psalm 141:3–4a)

Guide my steps by your word, so I will not be overcome by any evil. (Psalm 119:133)

May I make every effort to apply the benefits of his promises to my life. Then my faith will produce a life of moral excellence. A life of moral excellence leads to knowing God better. Knowing God leads to self-control. Self-control leads to patient endurance, and patient endurance leads to godliness. Godliness leads to love for other Christians, and finally I will grow to have genuine love for everyone. The more I grow like this, the more I will become productive and useful in my knowledge of my Lord Jesus Christ. (2 Peter 1:5–8)

I will not let sin control the way I live and not give in to its lustful desires. I will not let any part of my body become a tool of wickedness, to be used for sinning. Instead, I give myself completely to God since I have been given new life. And I use my whole body as a tool to do what is right for the glory of God. (Romans 6:12–13)

As a foreigner and an alien, here, may I keep away from evil desires because they fight against my very soul. (1 Peter 2:11)

When you follow the desires of your flesh, your lives will produce these evil results: sexual immorality, impure thoughts, eagerness for lustful pleasure, idolatry, participation in demonic activities, hostility, quarreling, jealousy, outbursts of anger, selfish ambition, divisions, the feeling that everyone is wrong except those in your own little group, envy, drunkenness, wild parties, and other kinds of sin. Let me tell you again, as I have before, that anyone living that sort of life will not inherit the Kingdom of God. But when the Holy Spirit controls our lives, he will produce this kind of fruit in us: love, joy, peace, patience, kindness, goodness, faithfulness, gentleness, and self-control. Here there is no conflict with the law. (Galatians 5:19–23)

May I get rid of all the filth and evil in my life, and humbly accept the message God has planted in my heart, for it is strong enough to save my soul. And may I remember, it is a message to obey, not just to listen to. If I don't obey, I am only fooling myself. (James 1:21–22)

If I let the Spirit direct my life, I will not satisfy the desires of the human nature. For what my human nature wants is opposed to what the Spirit wants and what the Spirit wants is opposed to what my human nature wants. These two are enemies, and this means I cannot do what I want to do. If the Spirit leads me, then I am not subject to the law. (Galatians 5:16–18)

Pause here to express any additional personal requests, especially concerning spiritual insight:

> Understanding and insight into the Word
> Understanding my identity in Christ
> Where I came from
> Who I am
> Where I am going
> Understanding God's purpose for my life
> My activities for this day
> Special concerns

Concerns for Others

Lord, I now prepare my heart for intercessory prayer for believers.

May your love for each other overflow more and more, and may you keep on growing in your knowledge and understanding. For I want you to understand what really matters, so that you may live pure and blameless lives until Christ returns. May you always be filled with the fruit of your salvation—those good things that are produced in your life by Jesus Christ—for this will bring much glory and praise to God. (Philippians 1:9–11)

I pray that all is well with you and that your body is as healthy as I know your soul is. (3 John 2)

In the spirit of these passages, I pray for:

> Personal friends
> Those in ministry
> Those who are oppressed and in need
> Special concerns

Prayer of Thanksgiving

For who you are and for what you have done, accept my thanks, Lord:

Those who live in the shelter of the Most High will find rest in the shadow of the Almighty. This I declare of the LORD: He alone is my refuge, my place of safety; he is my God, and I am trusting him. (Psalm 91:1–2)

The LORD is my light and my salvation—so why should I be afraid? The LORD protects me from danger—so why should I tremble? (Psalm 27:1)

Lord, thank you that you have made these promises:

For you who fear my name, the Sun of Righteousness will rise with healing in his wings. And you will go free, leaping with joy like calves let out to pasture. (Malachi 4:2)

You will rescue those who love you. You will protect those who trust in your name. When I call on you, you will answer; you will be with me in trouble. You will rescue me and honor me. You will satisfy me with a long life and give me your salvation. (Psalm 91:14–16)

Pause to offer your own expressions of thanksgiving.

Concluding Prayer

Surely your goodness and unfailing love will pursue me all the days of my life, and I will live in the house of the LORD forever. (Psalm 23:6)

Blessing and honor and glory and power belong to the one sitting on the throne and to the Lamb forever and ever. (Revelation 5:13)

And now, may the God of peace, who brought again from the dead our Lord Jesus, equip me with all I need for doing his will. May he produce in me, through the power of Jesus Christ, all that is pleasing to him. Jesus is the great Shepherd of the sheep by an everlasting covenant, signed with his blood. To him be glory forever and ever. Amen. (Hebrews 13:20–21)

Wednesday

Praise and Worship

Taste and see that the LORD is good. Oh, the joys of those who trust in him! Let the LORD's people show him reverence, for those who honor him will have all they need. (Psalm 34:8–9)

Thank you for making me so wonderfully complex! Your workmanship is marvelous—and how well I know it. (Psalm 139:14)

All of your works will thank you, LORD, and your faithful followers will bless you. They will talk together about the glory of your kingdom; they will celebrate examples of your power. They will tell about your mighty deeds and about the majesty and glory of your reign. For your kingdom is an everlasting kingdom. You rule generation after generation. The LORD is faithful in all he says; he is gracious in all he does. (Psalm 145:10–13)

David praised the LORD in the presence of the whole assembly: "O LORD, the God of our ancestor Israel, may you be praised forever and ever! Yours, O LORD, is the greatness, the power, the glory, the victory, and the majesty. Everything in the heavens and on earth is yours, O LORD, and this is your kingdom. We adore you as the one who is over all things. Riches and honor come from you alone, for you rule over everything. Power and might are in your hand, and it is at your discretion that people are made great and given strength. O our God, we thank you and praise your glorious name!" (1 Chronicles 29:10–13)

Pause to express your thoughts of praise and worship.

Personal Examination

God is so wise and so mighty. Who has ever challenged him successfully? (Job 9:4)

Oh, what joy for those whose rebellion is forgiven, whose sin is put out of sight! Yes, what joy for those whose record the LORD has cleared of sin, whose lives are lived in complete honesty! When I refused to confess my sin, I was weak and miserable, and I groaned all day long. Day and night your hand of discipline was heavy on me. My strength evaporated like water in the summer heat. Finally, I confessed all my sins to you and stopped trying to hide them. I said to myself, "I will confess my rebellion to the LORD." And you forgave me! All my guilt is gone. (Psalm 32:1–5)

Come, let us return to the LORD! He has torn us in pieces; now he will heal us. He has injured us; now he will bandage our wounds. In just a short time, he will restore us so we can live in his presence. (Hosea 6:1–2)

Ask the Spirit to search your heart and reveal any areas of unconfessed sin. Acknowledge these to the Lord and thank him for his forgiveness.

I—yes, I alone—am the one who blots out your sins for my own sake and will never think of them again. (Isaiah 43:25)

The Sovereign LORD, the Holy One of Israel, says, "Only in returning to me and waiting for me will you be saved. In quietness and confidence is your strength." (Isaiah 30:15)

Commitment

Lord, renew me by your Spirit as I offer these prayers to you:

May I not treat your holy name as common and ordinary. I must treat you as holy. It is you, the LORD, who makes me holy. (Leviticus 22:32)

May I be a person who really expects him to answer, for a doubtful mind is as unsettled as a wave of the sea that is driven and tossed by the wind. They can't make up their minds. They waver back and forth in everything they do. (James 1:6, 8)

May I continue to trust in the Lord Jesus and love all of God's people. (Philemon 5)

May I be strong with the special favor God gives me in Christ Jesus. (2 Timothy 2:1)

Pause to add your own prayers for personal renewal.

Personal Concerns

*Father, using your Word as a guide, I offer you my prayers
concerning my love for others.
Concerning love, you have said:*

"You must love the Lord your God with all your heart,
all your soul, and all your mind. This is the first and
greatest commandment. A second is equally important:
Love your neighbor as yourself. All the other commandments and all the demands of the prophets are based on
these two commandments." (Matthew 22:37–40)

May I do for others what I would like them to do for
me. This is a summary of all that is taught in the law
and the prophets. (Matthew 7:12)

Love is patient and kind. Love is not jealous or boastful
or proud or rude. Love does not demand its own way.
Love is not irritable, and it keeps no record of when it
has been wronged. It is never glad about injustice but
rejoices whenever the truth wins out. Love never gives
up, never loses faith, is always hopeful, and endures
through every circumstance. Love will last forever, but
prophecy and speaking in unknown languages and
special knowledge will all disappear. (1 Corinthians
13:4–8)

May I love my enemies and pray for those who persecute
me. (Matthew 5:44)

May I follow God's example in everything I do, because
I am his dear child. May I live a life filled with love for
others, following the example of Christ, who loved me

and gave himself as a sacrifice to take away my sins. And God was pleased, because that sacrifice was like sweet perfume to him. (Ephesians 5:1–2)

May I worship Christ as Lord of my life. And if I am asked about my Christian hope, I will always be ready to explain it. (1 Peter 3:15)

I should live wisely among those who are not Christians, and make the most of every opportunity, letting my conversation be gracious and effective so that I will have the right answer for everyone. (Colossians 4:5–6)

The kind of fasting I want calls you to free those who are wrongly imprisoned and to stop oppressing those who work for you. Treat them fairly and give them what they earn. I want you to share your food with the hungry and to welcome poor wanderers into your homes. Give clothes to those who need them, and do not hide from relatives who need your help. If you do these things, your salvation will come like the dawn. Yes, your healing will come quickly. Your godliness will lead you forward, and the glory of the LORD will protect you from behind. Then when you call, the LORD will answer. "Yes, I am here," he will quickly reply. (Isaiah 58:6–9)

May I not use foul or abusive language. May everything I say be good and helpful, so that my words will be an encouragement to those who hear them. May I not bring sorrow to God's Holy Spirit by whom I will be saved on the day of redemption. May I get rid of all bitterness, rage, anger, harsh words, and slander, as well as all types of malicious behavior. Instead, may I be kind to others, tenderhearted, and forgiving, just as God through Christ has forgiven me. (Ephesians 4:29–32)

May I not be selfish, living to make a good impression on others. May I be humble, thinking of others as better than myself. May I not think only about my own affairs, but be interested in others, too, and what they are doing. (Philippians 2:3–4)

May I be of one mind, full of sympathy toward others, loving others with a tender heart and a humble mind. May I not repay evil for evil and not retaliate when people say unkind things about me. Instead, I will pay them back with a blessing. That is what God wants me to do, and he will bless me for it. (1 Peter 3:8–9)

Pause here to express any additional personal requests, especially concerning relationships with others:

Greater love and compassion for others
Loved ones
Those who do not know Christ
Those in need
My activities for this day
Special concerns

Concerns for Others

Lord, I now prepare my heart for intercessory prayer for Christian witness.

May I devote myself to prayer with an alert mind and a thankful heart. May I not forget to pray, too, that God will give us many opportunities to preach about his secret plan. That is why I am here in chains. Pray that I will proclaim this message as clearly as I should. (Colossians 4:2–4)

I pray that you will give me the right words as I boldly explain your secret plan. (Ephesians 6:19)

In the spirit of these passages, I pray for those who do not know Christ:

Friends
Relatives
Neighbors
Co-workers
Special opportunities

Prayer of Thanksgiving

For who you are and for what you have done, accept my thanks, Lord:

All honor to the God and Father of our Lord Jesus Christ, for it is by his boundless mercy that God has given us the privilege of being born again. Now we live with a wonderful expectation because Jesus Christ rose again from the dead. For God has reserved a priceless inheritance for his children. It is kept in heaven for you, pure and undefiled, beyond the reach of change and decay. And God, in his mighty power, will protect you until you receive this salvation, because you are trusting him. It will be revealed on the last day for all to see. (1 Peter 1:3–5)

Whom have I in heaven but you? I desire you more than anything on earth. My health may fail, and my spirit may grow weak, but God remains the strength of my heart; he is mine forever. (Psalm 73:25–26)

Why am I discouraged? Why so sad? I will put my hope in God! I will praise him again—my Savior and my God! (Psalm 42:11)

I still dare to hope when I remember this: The unfailing love of the Lord never ends! By his mercies we have been kept from complete destruction. Great is his faithfulness; his mercies begin afresh each day. (Lamentations 3:21–23)

Pause to offer your own expressions of thanksgiving.

Concluding Prayer

May the words of my mouth and the thoughts of my heart be pleasing to you, O Lord, my rock and my redeemer. (Psalm 19:14)

Now glory be to God, who by his mighty power at work within us is able to accomplish infinitely more than we would ever dare to ask or hope. May he be given glory in the church and in Christ Jesus forever and ever through endless ages. Amen. (Ephesians 3:20–21)

Thursday

Praise and Worship

Praise the LORD! How good it is to sing praises to our God! How delightful and how right! (Psalm 147:1)

Praise the name of God forever and ever, for he alone has all wisdom and power. He determines the course of world events; he removes kings and sets others on the throne. He gives wisdom to the wise and knowledge to the scholars. He reveals deep and mysterious things and knows what lies hidden in darkness, though he himself is surrounded by light. God is wise and powerful! (Daniel 2:20–22)

O God, you are my God; I earnestly search for you. My soul thirsts for you; my whole body longs for you in this parched and weary land where there is no water. I have seen you in your sanctuary and gazed upon your power and glory. Your unfailing love is better to me than life itself; how I praise you! I will honor you as long as I live, lifting up my hands to you in prayer. You satisfy me more than the richest of foods. I will praise you with songs of joy. I lie awake thinking of you, meditating on you through the night. I think how much you have helped me; I sing for joy in the shadow of your protecting wings. I follow close behind you; your strong right hand holds me securely. (2 Samuel 22:47; Psalm 18:46)

Pause to express your thoughts of praise and worship.

Personal Examination

O LORD, do not rebuke me in your anger or discipline me in your rage. Have compassion on me, LORD, for I am weak. Heal me, LORD, for my body is in agony. I am sick at heart. How long, O LORD, until you restore me? (Psalm 6:1–3)

My destruction is sealed, for I am a sinful man and a member of a sinful race. Yet I have seen the King, the LORD Almighty! (Isaiah 6:5)

There is not a single person in all the earth who is always good and never sins. (Ecclesiastes 7:20)

I have sinned against the LORD, the God of Israel. (Joshua 7:20)

If I say I have no sin, I am only fooling myself and refusing to accept the truth. But if I confess my sins to him, he is faithful and just to forgive me and to cleanse me from every wrong. If I claim I have not sinned, I am calling God a liar and showing that his word has no place in my heart. (1 John 1:8–10)

Ask the Spirit to search your heart and reveal any areas of unconfessed sin. Acknowledge these to the Lord and thank him for his forgiveness.

I will sing to the LORD, all you godly ones! I will praise his holy name. His anger lasts for a moment, but his favor lasts a lifetime! Weeping may go on all night, but joy comes with the morning. (Psalm 30:4–5)

Commitment

Lord, renew me by your Spirit as I offer these prayers to you:

Choose to love the LORD your God and to obey him and commit yourself to him, for he is your life. Then you will live long in the land the LORD swore to give your ancestors Abraham, Isaac, and Jacob. (Deuteronomy 30:20)

You must be holy because I, the LORD, am holy. I have set you apart from all other people to be my very own. (Leviticus 20:26)

I have been born again. My new life did not come from my earthly parents because the life they gave me will end in death. But this new life will last forever because it comes from the eternal, living word of God. So may I get rid of all malicious behavior and deceit and not just pretend to be good! May I be done with hypocrisy and jealousy and backstabbing. (1 Peter 1:23; 2:1)

The heavenly Father to whom we pray has no favorites when he judges. He will judge or reward us according to what we do. So I must live in reverent fear of him during my time as a foreigner here on earth. (1 Peter 1:17)

Pause to add your own prayers for personal renewal.

Personal Concerns

Father, using your Word as a guide, I offer you my prayers concerning these practical exhortations.

May God, the glorious Father of our Lord Jesus Christ, give me spiritual wisdom and understanding, so that I might grow in my knowledge of God. I pray that my heart will be flooded with light so that I can understand the wonderful future he has promised to me. I want to realize what a rich and glorious inheritance he has given to me. I pray that I will begin to understand the incredible greatness of his power for me, because I believe him. This is the same mighty power that raised Christ from the dead and seated him in the place of honor at God's right hand in the heavenly realms. Now he is far above any ruler or authority or power or leader or anything else in this world or in the world to come. (Ephesians 1:17–21)

May I always be joyful and keep on praying. No matter what happens, I will always be thankful, for this is God's will for me, because I belong to Christ Jesus. May I test everything that is said, holding on to what is good and keeping away from every kind of evil. (1 Thessalonians 5:16–18, 21–22)

Whenever trouble comes my way, let it be an opportunity for me to be joyful. For when my faith is tested, my endurance has a chance to grow. So let it grow, for when my endurance is fully developed, I will be strong in character and ready for anything. If I need wisdom—when I want to know what God wants me to do—I will ask him, and he will gladly tell me. He will not resent my asking. (James 1:2–5)

346

May I be strong and steady, always enthusiastic about the Lord's work, for I know that nothing I do for the Lord is ever useless. (1 Corinthians 15:58)

May I be strong with the Lord's mighty power as I put on all of God's armor so that I will be able to stand firm against all strategies and tricks of the Devil. (Ephesians 6:10–11)

May I think clearly and exercise self-control. I look forward to the special blessings that will come to me at the return of Jesus Christ. As I obey God, may I not slip back into my old ways of doing evil; I didn't know any better then. But now I must be holy in everything I do, just as God—who chose me to be his child—is holy. For he himself has said, "You must be holy because I am holy." (1 Peter 1:13–16)

May I not worry about anything; instead, pray about everything. I will tell God what I need, and thank him for all he has done. If I do this, I will experience God's peace, which is far more wonderful than the human mind can understand. His peace will guard my heart and mind as I live in Christ Jesus. (Philippians 4:6–7)

May I fix my thoughts on what is true and honorable and right. May I think about things that are pure and lovely and admirable, things that are excellent and worthy of praise. (Philippians 4:8)

Pause here to express any additional personal requests, especially concerning faithfulness as a steward:

347

Of time
Of talents
Of treasure
Of truth
Of relationships
My activities for this day
Special concerns

Concerns for Others

Lord, I now prepare my heart for intercessory prayer for government.

We should pray for all people. As we make our requests, we plead for God's mercy upon them, and give thanks. We pray this way for kings and all others who are in authority, so that we can live in peace and quietness, in godliness and dignity. This is good and pleases God our Savior, for he wants everyone to be saved and to understand the truth. (1 Timothy 2:1–4)

In the spirit of this passage, I pray for:

Spiritual revival
Local government
State government
National government
Current events and concerns

Prayer of Thanksgiving

For who you are and for what you have done, accept my thanks, Lord:

Great is the LORD! He is most worthy of praise! He is to be revered above all gods. The gods of other nations are merely idols, but the LORD made the heavens! Honor and majesty surround him; strength and beauty are in his dwelling. O nations of the world, recognize the LORD, recognize that the LORD is glorious and strong. Give to the LORD the glory he deserves! Bring your offering and come to worship him. Worship the LORD in all his holy splendor. (1 Chronicles 16:25–29)

With Jesus' help, let us continually offer our sacrifice of praise to God by proclaiming the glory of his name. (Hebrews 13:15)

God is my refuge and strength, Always ready to help in times of trouble. (Psalm 46:1)

My heart rejoices in the LORD! Oh, how the LORD has blessed me! Now I have an answer for my enemies, as I delight in your deliverance.
No one is holy like you, LORD! There is no one besides you; there is no Rock like our God. (1 Samuel 2:1–2)

Pause to offer your own expressions of thanksgiving.

Concluding Prayer

The LORD keeps you from all evil and preserves your life. The LORD keeps watch over you as you come and go, both now and forever. (Psalm 121:7–8)

May the LORD bless you and protect you. May the LORD smile on you and be gracious to you. May the LORD show you his favor and give you his peace. (Numbers 6:24–26)

God, who gives me hope, will keep me happy and full of peace as I believe in him. May I overflow with hope through the power of the Holy Spirit. (Romans 15:13)

Friday

Praise and Worship

How great you are, O Sovereign LORD! There is no one like you, and there is no other God. (2 Samuel 7:22)

O LORD, God of our ancestors, you alone are the God who is in heaven. You are ruler of all the kingdoms of the earth. You are powerful and mighty; no one can stand against you! (2 Chronicles 20:6)

You are the fountain of life, the light by which we see. (Psalm 36:9)

Come, let us sing to the LORD! Let us give a joyous shout to the rock of our salvation! Let us come before him with thanksgiving. Let us sing him psalms of praise. For the LORD is a great God, the great King above all gods. Come, let us worship and bow down. Let us kneel before the LORD our maker, for he is our God. We are the people he watches over, the sheep under his care. Oh, that you would listen to his voice today! (Psalm 95:1–3, 6–7)

I will sing to the LORD as long as I live. I will praise my God to my last breath! May he be pleased by all these thoughts about him, for I rejoice in the LORD. (Psalm 104:33–34)

Pause to express your thoughts of praise and worship.

Personal Examination

From the depths of despair, O LORD, I call for your help. Hear my cry, O LORD. Pay attention to my prayer. LORD, if you kept a record of our sins, who, O LORD, could ever survive? But you offer forgiveness, that we might learn to fear you. (Psalm 130:1–4)

Every time you punished us you were being just. We have sinned greatly, and you gave us only what we deserved. (Nehemiah 9:33)

May I return to the LORD my God, for my sins have brought me down. May I bring my petitions, and return to the LORD. I will say to him, "Forgive all my sins and graciously receive me, so that I may offer you the sacrifice of praise." (Hosea 14:1–2)

Ask the Spirit to search your heart and reveal any areas of unconfessed sin. Acknowledge these to the Lord and thank him for his forgiveness.

The LORD is merciful and gracious; he is slow to get angry and full of unfailing love. He will not constantly accuse us, nor remain angry forever. He has not punished us for all our sins, nor does he deal with us as we deserve. For his unfailing love toward those who fear him is as great as the height of the heavens above the earth. He has removed our rebellious acts as far away from us as the east is from the west. The LORD is like a father to his children, tender and compassionate to those who fear him. For he understands how weak we are; he knows we are only dust. (Psalm 103:8–14)

Commitment

Lord, renew me by your Spirit as I offer these prayers to you:

Who is a faithful, sensible servant, to whom the master can give the responsibility of managing his household and feeding his family? If the master returns and finds that the servant has done a good job, there will be a reward. (Matthew 24:45–46)

May I keep alert and pray. Otherwise temptation will overpower me. For though the spirit is willing enough, the body is weak! (Matthew 26:41)

May I continue to live in fellowship with Christ so that when he returns, I will be full of courage and not shrink back from him in shame. (1 John 2:28)

May I be ready all the time, for the Son of Man will come when least expected. (Matthew 24:44; Luke 12:40)

Pause to add your own prayers for personal renewal.

Personal Concerns

Father, using your Word as a guide, I offer you my prayers concerning my need for wisdom.

I pray that from his glorious, unlimited resources he will give me mighty inner strength through his Holy Spirit. I pray that Christ will be more and more at home in my heart as I trust in him. May my roots go down deep into the soil of God's marvelous love. And may I have the power to understand, as all God's people should, how wide, how long, how high, and how deep his love really is. May I experience the love of Christ, though it is so great I will never fully understand it. Then I will be filled with the fullness of life and power that comes from God. (Ephesians 3:16–19)

If I have found favor with you, show me your intentions so I will understand you more fully and do exactly what you want me to do. (Exodus 33:13)

Whatever I do, may I do all for the glory of God. (1 Corinthians 10:31)

May I study your Book continually and meditate on it day and night so I may be sure to obey all that is written in it. Only then will I succeed. (Joshua 1:8)

I will study your commandments and reflect on your ways. I will delight in your principles and not forget your word. Be good to your servant, that I may live and obey your word. Open my eyes to see the wonderful truths in your law. (Psalm 119:15–18)

Let me be quick to listen, slow to speak, and slow to get angry. My anger can never make things right in God's sight. (James 1:19–20)

May I guard my heart, for it affects everything I do. May I avoid all perverse talk, staying far from corrupt speech. May I look straight ahead, fixing my eyes on what lies before me. I will mark out a straight path for my feet, stick to it and stay safe. May I not get sidetracked; keep my feet from following evil. (Proverbs 4:23–27)

I am the salt of the earth. But what good is salt if it has lost its flavor? Can you make it useful again? It will be thrown out and trampled underfoot as worthless. I am the light of the world—like a city on a mountain, glowing in the night for all to see. I won't hide my light under a basket! Instead, I will put it on a stand and let it shine for all. In the same way, I will let my good deeds shine out for all to see, so that everyone will praise my heavenly Father. (Matthew 5:13–16)

In everything I do, may I stay away from complaining and arguing, so that no one can speak a word of blame against me. May I live a clean, innocent life as a child of God in a dark world full of crooked and perverse people. Let my life shine brightly before you, holding tightly to the word of life, so that when Christ returns, I will be proud that I did not lose the race and that my work was not useless. (Philippians 2:14–16)

May I serve others in humility, for "God sets himself against the proud, but he shows favor to the humble." So may I humble myself under the mighty power of God, and in his good time he will honor me. I will give all my worries and cares to God, for he cares about what happens to me. (1 Peter 5:5–7)

Pause here to express any additional personal requests, especially concerning family and ministry:

Family
Ministry
Sharing Christ with others
Helping others grow in him
Career
My activities for this day
Special concerns

Concerns for Others

Lord, I now prepare my heart for intercessory prayer for missions.

Finally, dear brothers and sisters, I ask you to pray for us. Pray first that the Lord's message will spread rapidly and be honored wherever it goes, just as when it came to you. Pray, too, that we will be saved from wicked and evil people, for not everyone believes in the Lord. (2 Thessalonians 3:1–2)

The harvest is so great, but the workers are so few. Therefore, I will pray to the Lord who is in charge of the harvest, and ask him to send out more workers for his fields. (Matthew 9:37–38; Luke 10:2)

In the spirit of these passages, I pray for:

Local missions
National missions
World missions
The fulfillment of the Great Commission
Special concerns

Prayer of Thanksgiving

For who you are and for what you have done, accept my thanks, Lord:

I will thank you, LORD, with all my heart; I will tell of all the marvelous things you have done. I will be filled with joy because of you. I will sing praises to your name, O Most High. (Psalm 9:1–2)

Lord God Almighty, I give thanks to you, the one who is and who always was, for now you have assumed your great power and have begun to reign. (Revelation 11:17)

I will sing about your power. I will shout with joy each morning because of your unfailing love. For you have been my refuge, a place of safety in the day of distress. O my Strength, to you I sing praises, for you, O God, are my refuge, the God who shows me unfailing love. (Psalm 59:16–17)

Pause to offer your own expressions of thanksgiving.

Concluding Prayer

Teach me to make the most of my time, so that I may grow in wisdom. (Psalm 90:12)

A single day in your courts is better than a thousand anywhere else! I would rather be a gatekeeper in the house of my God than live the good life in the homes of the wicked. For the LORD God is our light and protector. He gives us grace and glory. No good thing will

357

the LORD withhold from those who do what is right. O LORD Almighty, happy are those who trust in you. (Psalm 84:10–12)

Glory and honor to God forever and ever. He is the eternal King, the unseen one who never dies; he alone is God. Amen. (1 Timothy 1:17)

Saturday

Praise and Worship

Praise the LORD, I tell myself; O LORD my God, how great you are! You are robed with honor and with majesty; you are dressed in a robe of light. You stretch out the starry curtain of the heavens. (Psalm 104:1–2)

Shout joyful praises to God, all the earth! Sing about the glory of his name! Tell the world how glorious he is. Say to God, "How awesome are your deeds! Your enemies cringe before your mighty power. Everything on earth will worship you; they will sing your praises, shouting your name in glorious songs." (Psalm 66:1–4)

The LORD is righteous in everything he does; he is filled with kindness. The LORD is close to all who call on him, yes, to all who call on him sincerely. He fulfills the desires of those who fear him; he hears their cries for help and rescues them. The LORD protects all those who love him, but he destroys the wicked. I will praise the LORD, and everyone on earth will bless his holy name forever and forever. (Psalm 145:17–21)

Pause to express your thoughts of praise and worship.

Personal Examination

Remember, O LORD, your unfailing love and compassion, which you have shown from long ages past. Forgive the rebellious sins of my youth; look instead through the eyes of your unfailing love, for you are merciful, O LORD. The LORD is good and does what is right; he shows the proper path to those who go astray. He leads the humble in what is right, teaching them his way. The LORD leads with unfailing love and faithfulness all those who keep his covenant and obey his decrees. For the honor of your name, O LORD, forgive my many, many sins. (Psalm 25:6–11)

O God, you know how foolish I am; my sins cannot be hidden from you. Don't let those who trust in you stumble because of me, O Sovereign LORD Almighty. Don't let me cause them to be humiliated, O God of Israel. (Psalm 69:5–6)

O LORD, have mercy on me; Heal me, for I have sinned against you. (Psalm 41:4)

O LORD, you alone can heal me; you alone can save. My praises are for you alone! (Jeremiah 17:14)

Ask the Spirit to search your heart and reveal any areas of unconfessed sin. Acknowledge these to the Lord and thank him for his forgiveness.

I will cleanse away their sins against me, and I will forgive all their sins. (Jeremiah 33:8)

Search me, O God, and know my heart; test me and know my thoughts. Point out anything in me that offends you, and lead me along the path of everlasting life. (Psalm 139:23–24)

Commitment

Lord, renew me by your Spirit as I offer these prayers to you:

I am the Lord's servant; I am willing to accept whatever he wants. (Luke 1:38)

The day of the Lord will come as unexpectedly as a thief. The heavens will pass away with a terrible noise, and everything in them will disappear in fire, and the earth and everything on it will be exposed to judgment. Since everything around us is going to melt away, I should be living a holy, godly life! I should look forward to that day and hurry it along—the day when God will set the heavens on fire and the elements will melt away in the flames. But I am looking forward to the new heavens and new earth he has promised, a world where everyone is right with God. And so while I am waiting for these things to happen, let me make every effort to live a pure and blameless life. And be at peace with God. (2 Peter 3:10–14)

May I stop just saying I love others; let me really show it by my actions. It is by my actions that I know I am living in the truth, so I will be confident when I stand before the Lord, even if my heart condemns me. For God is greater than my heart, and he knows everything. If my conscience is clear, I can come to God with bold confidence. And I will receive whatever I request because I obey him and do the things that please him. (1 John 3:18–22)

Put me on trial, LORD, and cross-examine me. Test my motives and affections. For I am constantly aware of your unfailing love, and I have lived according to your truth. (Psalm 26:2–3)

Pause to add your own prayers for personal renewal.

Personal Concerns

Father, using your Word as a guide, I offer you my prayers concerning my spiritual walk.

Since the Spirit has given me life, may he also control my life. (Galatians 5:25)

May God give me a complete understanding of what he wants to do in my life, and make me wise with spiritual wisdom. Then the way I live will always honor and please the Lord, and I will continually do good, kind things for others. All the while, I will learn to know God better and better, always thanking the Father, who has enabled me to share the inheritance that belongs to God's holy people, who live in the light. (Colossians 1:9–10, 12)

The LORD is our God, the LORD alone. And I must love the LORD my God with all my heart, all my soul, and all my strength. (Deuteronomy 6:4–5)

Do not worship any other gods besides me. Do not make idols of any kind, whether in the shape of birds or animals or fish. You must never worship or bow down to them, for I, the Lord your God, am a jealous God who will not share your affection with any other god! I do not leave unpunished the sins of those who hate me, but I punish the children for the sins of their parents to the third and fourth generations. But I lavish my love on those who love me and obey my commands, even for a thousand generations. Do not misuse the name of the Lord your God. The Lord will not let you go unpunished if you misuse his name. Observe the Sabbath day by keeping it holy, as the Lord your God has commanded you. Six days a week are set apart for your daily duties and regular work, but the seventh day is a day of rest dedicated to the Lord your God. On that day no one in your household may do any kind of work. This includes you, your sons and daughters, your male and female servants, your oxen and donkeys and other livestock, and any foreigners living among you. All your male and female servants must rest as you do. Remember that you were once slaves in Egypt and that the Lord your God brought you out with amazing power and mighty deeds. That is why the Lord your God has commanded you to observe the Sabbath day. Honor your father and mother, as the Lord your God commanded you. Then you will live a long, full life in the land the Lord your God will give you. Do not murder. Do not commit adultery. Do not steal. Do not testify falsely against your neighbor. Do not covet your neighbor's wife. Do not covet your neighbor's house or land, male or female servant, ox or donkey, or anything else your neighbor owns. (Exodus 20:3–17; Deuteronomy 5:7–21)

I am not fighting against people made of flesh and blood, but against the evil rulers and authorities of the unseen world, against those mighty powers of darkness who rule this world, and against wicked spirits in the heavenly realms. May I use every piece of God's armor to resist the enemy in the time of evil, so that after the battle I will still be standing firm. I will stand my ground, putting on the sturdy belt of truth and the body armor of God's righteousness. For shoes, I will put on the peace that comes from the Good News, so that I will be fully prepared. In every battle I will need faith as my shield to stop the fiery arrows aimed at me by Satan. I will put on salvation as my helmet, and take the sword of the Spirit, which is the word of God. I will pray at all times and on every occasion in the power of the Holy Spirit. May I stay alert and be persistent in my prayers for all Christians everywhere. (Ephesians 6:12–18)

May my love for others overflow more and more, and may I keep on growing in my knowledge and understanding. For I want to understand what really matters, so that I may live a pure and blameless life until Christ returns. May I always be filled with the fruit of my salvation—those good things that are produced in my life by Jesus Christ—for this will bring much glory and praise to God. (Philippians 1:9–11)

Since God chose me to be one of his holy people whom he loves, I must clothe myself with tenderhearted mercy, kindness, humility, gentleness, and patience. I must make allowance for other's faults and forgive the person who offends me. I remember, the Lord forgave me, so I must forgive others. And the most important piece of clothing I must wear is love. Love is what binds us all together in perfect harmony. And let the peace that comes from Christ rule in my heart. For as a member of one body I am called to live in peace and always be thankful. May the words of Christ, in all their richness, live in my heart and make me wise. May I use his words to teach and counsel others and sing psalms and hymns and spiritual songs to God with a thankful heart. And whatever I do or say, may it be as a representative of the Lord Jesus, while I give thanks through him to God the Father. (Colossians 3:12–17)

Since I am surrounded by such a huge crowd of witnesses to the life of faith, let me strip off every weight that slows me down, especially the sin that so easily hinders my progress. And let me run with endurance the race that God has set before me. May I do this by keeping my eyes on Jesus, on whom my faith depends from start to finish. He was willing to die a shameful death on the cross because of the joy he knew would be his afterward. Now he is seated in the place of highest honor beside God's throne in heaven. I will think about all he endured when sinful people did such terrible things to him, so that I don't become weary and give up. (Hebrews 12:1–3)

May I consider everything worthless when compared with the priceless gain of knowing Christ Jesus my Lord. I have discarded everything else, counting it all as garbage, so that I may have Christ and become one with him. I no longer count on my own goodness or my ability to obey God's law, but I trust Christ to save me. For God's way of making us right with himself depends on faith. As a result, I can really know Christ and experience the mighty power that raised him from the dead. I can learn what it means to suffer with him, sharing in his death. (Philippians 3:8–10)

I don't mean to say that I have already achieved things or that I have already reached perfection! But I keep working toward that day when I will finally be all that Christ Jesus saved me for and wants me to be. No, I am still not all I should be, but I am focusing all my energies on this one thing: forgetting the past and looking forward to what lies ahead, I strain to reach the end of the race and receive the prize for which God, through Christ Jesus, is calling us up to heaven. (Philippians 3:12–14)

May my faith prove far more precious to God than gold and remain strong after being tried by fiery trials. May it bring you much praise and glory and honor on the day when Jesus Christ is revealed to the whole world. (1 Peter 1:7)

Pause here to express any additional requests, especially these personal concerns:

Spiritual warfare
The world
The flesh
The devil
Growth in character
Personal disciplines
Physical health and strength
My activities for this day
Special concerns

Concerns for Others

Lord, I now prepare my heart for intercessory prayer for world affairs.

Our Father in heaven, may your name be honored. May your Kingdom come soon. May your will be done here on earth, just as it is in heaven. (Matthew 6:9–10)

The end of the world is coming soon. Therefore, we should be earnest and disciplined in our prayers. (1 Peter 4:7)

In the spirit of these passages, I pray for:

The poor and hungry
The oppressed and persecuted
Those in authority
Peace among nations
Current events and concerns

Prayer of Thanksgiving

For who you are and for what you have done, accept my thanks, O LORD: I will sing of the tender mercies of the LORD forever! Young and old will hear of your faithfulness. Your unfailing love will last forever. Your faithfulness is as enduring as the heavens. (Psalm 89:1–2)

Unfailing love and truth have met together. Righteousness and peace have kissed! Truth springs up from the earth, and righteousness smiles down from heaven. (Psalm 85:10–11)

As for me, I look to the LORD for his help. I wait confidently for God to save me, and my God will certainly hear me. (Micah 7:7)

Praise the LORD! For he has heard my cry for mercy. The LORD is my strength, my shield from every danger. I trust in him with all my heart. He helps me, and my heart is filled with joy. I burst out in songs of thanksgiving. (Psalm 28:6–7)

Pause to offer your own expressions of thanksgiving.

Concluding Prayer

Dear brothers and sisters, I close my letter with these last words: Rejoice. Change your ways. Encourage each other. Live in harmony and peace. Then the God of love and peace will be with you. May the grace of our Lord Jesus Christ, the love of God, and the fellowship of the Holy Spirit be with you all. (2 Corinthians 13:11, 13)

Blessing and glory and wisdom and thanksgiving and honor and power and strength belong to our God forever and forever. Amen! (Revelation 7:12)

May our Lord Jesus Christ and God our Father, who loved us and in his special favor gave us everlasting comfort and good hope, comfort our hearts and give us strength in every good thing we do and say. (2 Thessalonians 2:16–17)

Perspectives on Prayer

Prayer catapults us onto the frontier of the spiritual life. It is original research in unexplored territory.

Richard Foster

The church has many organizers, but few agonizers; many who pay, but few who pray; many resters, but few wrestlers; many who are enterprising, but few who are interceding. People who are not praying are playing. . . . Two prerequisites of dynamic Christian living are vision and passion, and both of these are generated in the prayer closet. The ministry of preaching is open to a few. The ministry of praying is open to every child of God.

Leonard Ravenhill

∞♦∞

The concept of communicating with God, of talking directly and openly with him just as we would talk with an intimate friend, is one of the great truths of Scripture.

Prayer is a phenomenal privilege, yet many people associate prayer with the word "boredom." It is a yawn word to them: "Well, I guess we'll have to pray. . . ." For others, the conception of prayer never gets beyond the level of "help" and "gimme." They resort to prayer when they want God to bail them out or to fulfill their cravings.

The biblical portrait of prayer is far more dynamic than these misconceptions, and the more we learn about the principles and power of prayer, the more we will be motivated to cultivate this aspect of our relationship with God.

Prayer is the prelude to all effective ministry. It has been said that "Satan laughs at our toiling, mocks our wisdom, but trembles when he sees the weakest saint on his knees." The real spiritual battle is won on the field of prayer; ministry simply claims the territory that has been gained. When prayer is overlooked or appended as an afterthought to service, the power of God is often absent. It is dangerously easy to move away from dependence upon God and to slip into the trap of self-reliance.

What Is Prayer?

Simply defined, prayer is a dialogue between God and man. It is "an intimate conversation of the pious with God" (John Calvin). Prayer often involves individual and group needs (Matthew 14:30; Daniel 9:3–19) and concerns (Habakkuk 1:1–4; 12–17). However, "true prayer is not asking in itself, but the relationship of friendship with God, in which asking and receiving is simply part of the outcome" (J. A. Hanne).

Because it is part of a relationship, prayer involves a dialogue, not merely a monologue. While God wants us to talk to him about our problems, plans, and concerns, there are also times when we should be silent before him so that we can be sensitive and receptive to his desires and direction. Prayerful meditation upon a text of Scripture is an especially helpful way to listen to God.

Prayer is a spiritual resource which triggers the supernatural. It is an effective weapon when unsheathed, but too often it remains in the scabbard. Prayer and action are complimentary, not contradictory, and it is wise to overlap them as much as possible. Christian service is most effective when prayer not only precedes it but also flows together with it.

The gift of open communication with God and immediate access to him is one of the great benefits of the salvation Jesus purchased for us. An infinite and holy God could never commune with sinful and rebellious creatures. It is the goodness, the grace, and the love of God, most clearly seen in the person and work of Christ, that brought all who have trusted in him into a position they could never hope to earn.

That is why we have a great High Priest who has gone to heaven, Jesus the Son of God. Let us cling to him and never stop trusting him. This High Priest of ours

373

understands our weaknesses, for he faced all of the same temptations we do, yet he did not sin. *So let us come* boldly to the throne of our gracious God. There we will receive his mercy, and we will find grace to help us when we need it.

Hebrews 4:14–16

And so, dear brothers and sisters, we can boldly enter heaven's Most Holy Place because of the blood of Jesus. This is the new, life-giving way that Christ has opened up for us through the sacred curtain, by means of his death for us. And since we have a great High Priest who rules over God's people, *let us go right into the presence of God,* with true hearts fully trusting him. For our evil consciences have been sprinkled with Christ's blood to make us clean, and our bodies have been washed with pure water. Without wavering, let us hold tightly to the hope we say we have, for God can be trusted to keep his promise.

Hebrews 10:19–23

Because of the grace that has been lavished upon us and the free access we have been given to the Father (Ephesians 2:18), we have the opportunity and the responsibility to come to God, drawing near to him in all times of need. "If you sinful people know how to give good gifts to your children, how much more will your heavenly Father give good gifts to those who ask him." (Matthew 7:11).

Why Should We Pray?

1. *Prayer enhances our fellowship and intimacy with God.* "I love the LORD because he hears and answers

374

my prayers. Because he bends down and listens, I will pray as long as I have breath!" (Psalm 116:1–2). "The LORD, the Maker of the heavens and earth—the LORD is his name—says this: Ask me and I will tell you some remarkable secrets about what is going to happen here." (Jeremiah 33:2–3).

2. *The Scriptures command us to pray.* "One day Jesus told his disciples a story to illustrate their need for constant prayer and to show them that they must never give up" (Luke 18:1). "Pray at all times and on every occasion in the power of the Holy Spirit. Stay alert and be persistent in your prayers for all Christians everywhere" (Ephesians 6:18). "Always be joyful. Keep on praying. No matter what happens, always be thankful, for this is God's will for you who belong to Christ Jesus" (1 Thessalonians 5:16–18). "I urge you, first of all, to pray for all people. As you make your requests, plead for God's mercy upon them, and give thanks" (1 Timothy 2:1).

3. *When we pray, we follow the example of Christ and other great people in Scripture like Moses and Elijah.* "The next morning Jesus awoke long before daybreak and went out alone into the wilderness to pray" (Mark 1:35). "The people screamed to Moses for help; and when he prayed to the LORD, the fire stopped" (Numbers 11:2). "At the customary time for offering the evening sacrifice, Elijah the prophet walked up to the altar and prayed, 'O LORD, God of Abraham, Isaac, and Jacob, prove today that you are God in Israel and that I am your servant. Prove that I have done all this at your command. O LORD, answer me! Answer me so these people will know that you, O LORD, are God and that you have brought them back to yourself" (1 Kings

18:36–37). "The earnest prayer of a righteous person has great power and wonderful results" (James 5:16; cf. 5:17–18).

4. *Prayer appropriates God's power for our lives.* In prayer, God allows us to participate with him in the accomplishment of his purposes and demonstration of his power. "Yes, I am the vine; you are the branches. Those who remain in me, and I in them, will produce much fruit. For apart from me you can do nothing" (John 15:5). "After this prayer, the building where they were meeting shook, and they were all filled with the Holy Spirit. And they preached God's message with boldness" (Acts 4:31; cf. Ephesians 3:16; Colossians 4:2–4).

5. *We receive special help from God when we pray.* "So let us come boldly to the throne of our gracious God. There we will receive his mercy, and we will find grace to help us when we need it" (Hebrews 4:16).

6. *Prayer makes a genuine difference.* God uses it to change people and shape history (Luke 11:9–10; James 5:16–18). "When I pray, coincidences happen; when I don't, they don't" (William Temple).

7. *Prayer develops our understanding and knowledge of God* (Psalm 37:3–6; 63:1–8; Ephesians 1:16–19). In it we acknowledge our dependence upon him for all our spiritual, emotional, intellectual, and physical needs so that we continue to trust him for everything. "In prayer, real prayer, we begin to think God's thoughts after Him: to desire the things He desires, to love the things He loves" (Richard Foster). "Prayer—secret, fervent, believing prayer—lies at the root of all personal godliness" (William Carey).

8. *Our prayers and God's answers give us joy and peace in our hearts* (John 16:23–24; Philippians 4:6–7). Our

problems may not disappear, but in prayer we gain a new perspective on our problems along with the peace and patience to stand firm.

9. *Prayer helps us understand and accomplish God's purposes for our lives.* This was what Paul desired for the Colossians: "So we have continued praying for you ever since we first heard about you. We ask God to give you a complete understanding of what he wants to do in your lives, and we ask him to make you wise with spiritual wisdom. Then the way you live will always honor and please the Lord, and you will continually do good, kind things for others. All the while, you will learn to know God better and better. We also pray that you will be strengthened with his glorious power so that you will have all the patience and endurance you need" (Colossians 1:9–11). "Spiritual power is not the power of prayer, but the power of God realized in action through a man in the attitude of prayer" (J. A. Hanne).

10. *Prayer changes our attitudes and desires* (2 Corinthians 12:7–9). In prayer we acknowledge the greatness of God's character and our desire to become more conformed to his character. We also acknowledge that in his wisdom he works all the things that happen in our lives together for our good (Romans 8:28). "Prayer keeps us trusting God for everything, opens the way for the Holy Spirit to transform us into the image of Jesus, and enables God to touch the lives of others whom we meet" (David Watson).

How Did Jesus Pray?

Prayer was an indispensable part of Jesus' life and ministry on earth. He never got too busy to talk with

377

his Father. This attitude of complete dependency and constant communication was the key to his fulfillment of everything he came to accomplish.

As he taught his disciples, Jesus provided a model for prayer which was recorded in two of the Gospels (Matthew 6:9–13 and Luke 11:1–4). He told his disciples to pray "in this way" (Matthew 6:9a), and a number of valuable principles can be gleaned from this model prayer:

"Our Father"

Accentuate God's Priority—Our prayers should concern God's interests first and our interests second. Compare Matthew 6:9–10 with Matthew 6:11–13.

Address God as Father—We can address our prayers directly to the Father because of the personal relationship with him that was made available to us through the work of Christ. We have become sons and daughters of the king through faith in his Son (John 1:12; 14:6; Galatians 3:26; Hebrews 10:19–22).

"Who Art in Heaven"

Affirm God's Supremacy—While it is true that we are in God's family, it is also true that our God is the sovereign, infinite Creator who is gloriously enthroned in heaven.

"Hallowed Be Thy Name"

Acclaim God as Holy and Righteous—To hallow means to honor, exalt, or glorify. Our concern in prayer must not only be the what, why, and how, but especially the *who*. Our prayers should include praise for God in terms of who he is and what he has done (Psalm 34:1–3; Isaiah

378

40:12–26; 43:1–21). We are called to fear, reverence, glorify, and magnify his holy name (John 17:6, 11, 12).

"Thy Kingdom Come"

Acknowledge God's Right to Rule—God's kingdom is
the sphere over which he rules, including his purposes for
the world in general and the body of Christ in particular.
We are to pray that God will bring about his rule of righteousness and justice on the earth, with Jesus Christ as
the ruler (2 Samuel 7:10–16; Luke 18:7–8). When we
pray for the coming of the kingdom, we are also praying
for the coming of the King (Revelation 22:20).

"Thy Will Be Done, on Earth as It Is in Heaven"

Assent to God's Will—We should pray that God's will
be accomplished on earth in the same way as it is by
the angelic host of heaven (Psalm 103:19–21). On the
personal level, this means that we are making ourselves
available for God to accomplish his will through us as
Jesus did during his earthly life (Matthew 26:39).

"Give Us This Day Our Daily Bread"

Ask for God's Provision—In prayer we acknowledge
that everything we have is a gift from God (James 1:17),
as we turn to him for the supply of our daily needs. God
has promised to provide our basic needs (Philippians
4:19), but not necessarily our wants.

"And Forgive Us Our Debts"

Admit the Need for God's Forgiveness—Our needs are
not only physical but spiritual. While it is true that all of
our sins were forgiven when we received Christ as our Sav-

ior (Ephesians 1:7; Colossians 2:13; Hebrews 10:14–18), we did not become perfect in our practice. When we sin, we must acknowledge it to God who will forgive and cleanse us from all unrighteousness (1 John 1:9).

"As We also Have Forgiven Our Debtors"

Accept God's Mandate to Forgive Others—Having experienced God's forgiveness, we are obligated to have a forgiving spirit toward others. We do not merit God's forgiveness by forgiving others; we mirror it (Matthew 18:21–35; Mark 11:25; Ephesians 4:32; Colossians 3:13).

"And Do Not Lead Us into Temptation"

Adhere to God in the Midst of Adversity—God does not *tempt* anyone to sin (James 1:13), but he does *test* the quality of our faith to stimulate us to grow in our relationship with him (Genesis 22:1; Rom. 5:3–5; James 1:2–4). God is willing and able to deliver us from every temptation as we turn to him (Luke 22:40; 1 Corinthians 10:13).

"But Deliver Us from Evil"

Actively Stand with God against the Evil One—We are to stand firm in the spiritual warfare by exercising our resources in Christ (Ephesians 6:10–18) and praying that God will deliver us from the wiles of the adversary (1 Peter 5:8–9). In the life of our Lord, prayer was not so much something he did as it was a relationship He maintained. It was the complete involvement of his mind, will, and emotions with his Father.

The tragedy of our day is not unanswered prayer but unoffered prayer.

J. Sidlow Baxter

Men may spurn our appeals, reject our message, oppose our arguments, despise our persons, but they are helpless against our prayers.

J. Sidlow Baxter

The Christian on his knees sees more than the philosopher on tiptoe.

Dwight L. Moody

Keep praying, but be thankful that God's answers are wiser than your prayers!

William Culbertson

Prayer is a powerful thing, for God has bound and tied Himself thereto. None can believe how powerful prayer is, and what it is able to effect, but those who have learned it by experience.

Martin Luther

Prayer is not an argument with God to persuade Him to move things our way, but an exercise by which we are enabled by His Spirit to move ourselves His way.

Leonard Ravenhill

There is not in the world a kind of life more sweet and delightful than that of a continual conversation with God.

Brother Lawrence

Kenneth Boa is engaged in a ministry of relational evangelism and discipleship, teaching, writing, and speaking. He holds a B.S. from Case Institute of Technology, a Th.M. from Dallas Theological Seminary, a Ph.D. from New York University, and a D.Phil. from the University of Oxford in England.

Dr. Boa is the president of Reflections Ministries, an organization that seeks to encourage, teach, and equip people to know Christ, follow him, become progressively conformed to his image, and reproduce his life in others. He is also president of Trinity House Publishers, a publishing company that is dedicated to the creation of tools that will help people manifest eternal values in a temporal arena by drawing them to intimacy with God and a better understanding of the culture in which they live.

Recent publications by Dr. Boa include *Conformed to His Image*, *20 Compelling Evidences that God Exists*, *Face to Face*, and *Faith Has Its Reasons*. He is a contributing editor to *The Open Bible* and *The Leadership Bible*, and the consulting editor of the *NASB Study Bible*.

Kenneth Boa also writes a free monthly teaching letter called *Reflections*. If you would like to be on the mailing list, visit www.reflectionsministries.org or call 800-DRAW NEAR (800-372-9632).

The Heart of God by Kenneth Boa is published in partnership with World Vision. Some of the proceeds from the purchase of this book support World Vision's mission. World Vision is a Christian relief and development organization dedicated to helping children and their communities worldwide reach their potential by tackling the causes of poverty. Motivated by their faith in Jesus, they serve the poor—regardless of a person's religion, race, ethnicity, or gender—as a demonstration of God's unconditional love for all people.

BakerBooks